Tax Policy Reforms 2018

OECD AND SELECTED PARTNER ECONOMIES

OECD

BETTER POLICIES FOR BETTER LIVES

This work is published under the responsibility of the Secretary-General of the OECD. The opinions expressed and arguments employed herein do not necessarily reflect the official views of OECD member countries.

This document, as well as any data and any map included herein, are without prejudice to the status of or sovereignty over any territory, to the delimitation of international frontiers and boundaries and to the name of any territory, city or area.

Please cite this publication as:
OECD (2018), *Tax Policy Reforms 2018: OECD and Selected Partner Economies*, OECD Publishing, Paris.
https://doi.org/10.1787/9789264304468-en

ISBN 978-92-64-30445-1 (print)
ISBN 978-92-64-30446-8 (PDF)

The statistical data for Israel are supplied by and under the responsibility of the relevant Israeli authorities. The use of such data by the OECD is without prejudice to the status of the Golan Heights, East Jerusalem and Israeli settlements in the West Bank under the terms of international law.

Photo credits: Cover image word cloud ©Tagul.com

Corrigenda to OECD publications may be found on line at: *www.oecd.org/about/publishing/corrigenda.htm*.

Foreword

This is the third edition of *Tax Policy Reforms: OECD and Selected Partner Economies*, which is an annual publication that provides comparative information on tax reforms across countries and tracks tax policy developments over time. The report covers the latest tax policy reforms in all OECD countries,[1] as well as in Argentina, Indonesia and South Africa.

This report was produced by the Tax Policy and Statistics Division of the OECD's Centre for Tax Policy and Administration. It was led by Sarah Perret and written jointly with Véronique Salins (Economics Department), Johanna Arlinghaus, Stéphane Buydens, Tibor Hanappi and Sean Kennedy (Centre for Tax Policy and Administration), under the supervision of Bert Brys. The authors would like to thank the delegates of Working Party No.2 on Tax Policy Analysis and Tax Statistics and the Committee on Fiscal Affairs for their inputs. The authors would also like to acknowledge Piet Battiau, Sveinbojrn Blondal, David Bradbury, Giorgia Maffini, David O'Sullivan, Nigel Pain, Alvaro Pereira, Pascal Saint-Amans, Michael Sharratt, Carrie Tyler, Kurt Van Dender, and Karena Garnier as well as the country desks of the OECD Economics Department for their support and valuable comments.

Table of contents

Tables

Figures

Boxes

Editorial

With monetary policy starting to return to normal in many countries, support provided by fiscal policy, including to a large extent through tax policy, has become more significant. Many countries have eased their fiscal stance to stimulate the economy by lowering taxes, increasing government spending, or both. This year's report highlights that the focus of the most recent tax reforms has been on cutting taxes on businesses and individuals with a view to boosting investment, consumption and labour market participation, continuing a trend that started a couple of years ago.

Among the countries that introduced the most significant tax reforms were a number of countries where tax reform was long overdue. The United States introduced the most sweeping tax reform, which completely overhauled its tax system, including both business and personal taxes. The year 2018 also saw the entry into force of significant tax reform packages in Argentina, France and Latvia. Broad tax reform packages are consistent with the view that tax systems should be considered as a whole and that, as opposed to looking at tax policies in isolation, the focus should be on the efficiency and equity effects of the overall tax system.

Other countries have introduced tax measures in a more piecemeal fashion, but many of these measures are a step in the right direction. A number of countries have sought to encourage greater labour market participation, most notably through the expansion of earned income tax credits. Efforts have also been made to broaden tax bases and to continue the fight against international corporate tax avoidance, in line with the commitments made by countries to implement the minimum standards and recommendations agreed upon as part of the OECD/G20 Base Erosion and Profit Shifting (BEPS) project. Administrative improvements and anti-fraud measures, in particular in the area of VAT, were also among the measures commonly adopted to enhance efficiency and collect greater tax revenues.

Going forward, however, greater action and coordination will be needed to avoid certain risks:

With global economic growth now closer to longer-term norms, the need for additional short-term fiscal stimulus is significantly lower. Fiscal policy choices should avoid the risk of excessive pro-cyclicality and be focused on medium-term challenges. Despite being on a declining trend, public debt and deficit levels remain high in many countries. As economic times improve, there is an opportunity to rebuild fiscal buffers, which will ultimately give more room for policy stimulus in the event of any future downturn. The focus of tax reforms should also shift to supporting the longer-term drivers of growth and equity. In this context, it is particularly important that tax reforms be financed in a manner that ensures their long-term sustainability.

Continued cooperation will also be important to prevent harmful tax competition. So far, while the declining trend in the average OECD corporate tax rate has gained renewed momentum since the crisis, corporate tax rate reductions are still less pronounced than before the crisis. Besides, the countries that introduced corporate tax rate cuts in 2018 included some of the countries that had the highest tax rates in 2017. If anything, these countries appear to be engaged in a "race to the average" rather than in a "race to the bottom", with their recent corporate tax rate cuts now placing them in the middle of the pack. There will be much interest in observing how countries respond to this trend in the future.

The report also highlights the crucial need to continue addressing equity issues and environmental challenges, which remain significant despite progress in recent years.

Tax policies should continue to focus on inclusiveness to ensure that improvements in incomes and standards of living are shared widely across the population. This is especially true in a context where positive developments in terms of employment are being overshadowed by wage stagnation, especially for low-wage workers. While there have been continued cuts in personal income taxes for low and middle-income earners, these have typically been small. In general, there is still ample scope to strengthen inclusiveness through tax systems, in particular by continuing to lower-labour tax wedges on low and middle-income workers, removing tax expenditures that disproportionately benefit the wealthy, and ensuring the effective taxation of personal capital income. Efforts to partly shift the financing of welfare systems from social security contributions towards general taxation could also be pursued further. Identifying the winners and losers of tax reforms and adequately compensating those who will lose out from new tax measures, particularly where they are at the bottom of the income and wealth distribution forms part of an inclusive tax agenda.

Progress on environmental taxation is urgently needed. While some progress has been achieved regarding the taxation of energy use, recent tax increases have not been meaningful enough to encourage significant carbon abatement outside of road transport. Aligning energy prices with the costs of climate change and air pollution is a central element of a cost-effective environmental policy. More generally, an increased emphasis should be placed on environmental taxation to encourage changes in behaviour that deliver improved environmental outcomes and help raise the levels of revenue collected from green taxes, which can be used to finance cuts in more distortive taxes.

Pascal Saint-Amans
Director, OECD Centre for Tax Policy and Administration

Executive summary

The year 2018 saw the entry into force of significant tax reforms in Argentina, France, Latvia and the United States. The focus of these reforms has largely been on supporting investment, through lower corporate taxes but also through changes in taxes on property and personal capital income. Some elements of these reforms are also aimed at enhancing fairness by lowering taxes on low and middle-income earners. However, none of these reforms are expected to be revenue-neutral. In addition, Belgium has introduced a comprehensive corporate income tax (CIT) reform, combining a significant reduction in the CIT rate with substantial base broadening.

The report identifies more broadly a number of common tax reform trends across the countries covered in the report:

- Personal income tax (PIT) cuts on labour income have continued, primarily to alleviate the tax burden on low and middle-income earners. One pattern of reform has been to increase earned income tax credits (EITCs), which have the potential to improve labour market participation and enhance PIT progressivity. In parallel, the trend towards higher tax rates on personal capital income has persisted, although some countries have expanded tax reliefs for some forms of financial income. From a country perspective, the most significant reforms were introduced in the United States with changes in PIT rates and deductions, Latvia with the introduction of a progressive PIT system, and France with a new flat tax on personal capital income.
- Regarding social security contributions (SSCs), reforms have generally been limited and SSCs will continue to weigh heavily on labour income in many countries. Compared to recent years, one development across countries has been a greater focus on SSC rate increases and base narrowing, which suggests that greater contributions will be placed upon a smaller number of contributors in some countries.
- This year has also seen an acceleration in CIT rate cuts, which has largely been driven by a few large economies, including countries with traditionally high corporate tax rates. Other notable base narrowing reforms, including the expansion of depreciation allowances, have also been aimed at supporting investment. Compared to previous years, very limited changes have been made to R&D and innovation-related tax incentives.
- Efforts to protect the CIT base against international tax avoidance have continued through anti-avoidance measures and the implementation of the OECD/G20 Base Erosion and Profit Shifting (BEPS) package, but these efforts have varied across countries.
- The taxation of highly digitalised businesses has become a major concern for many countries. Wide disparities in views across countries have prevented the adoption of a common approach so far and spurred the introduction of heterogeneous measures, creating a risk of increased complexity and uncertainty.

- Value-added tax (VAT) rates have stabilised, but increased revenues are expected from significant tax administration and anti-fraud measures in a number of countries. South Africa is the only country where the standard VAT rate was raised in 2018. High VAT rates have led many countries to look for alternative ways of raising additional VAT revenues, through base broadening – by removing or scaling back reduced VAT rates – and administrative and anti-fraud measures. Some of these measures, in particular split payments and the expansion of the domestic reverse charge mechanism, imply major changes to the way VAT has traditionally been collected. In some countries, reduced VAT rates have been expanded to address fairness concerns or to support specific industry sectors, although evidence shows that these tend to be poorly targeted policy instruments.
- New excise taxes are being introduced to deter harmful consumption, in addition to continued increases in excise duty rates on tobacco and alcohol. Some of the most notable reforms include new taxes on sugar-sweetened beverages in Ireland, South Africa and the United Kingdom, and the introduction of a tax on cannabis in Canada.
- Environmentally-related tax reforms have continued to focus on energy taxes but efforts have been made to go beyond road transport. While these changes go in the right direction, they have occurred only in a few countries and more significant reforms will be needed to align energy tax rates with environmental costs and generate additional tax revenues. Changes to vehicle taxes to encourage the use of cleaner vehicles have continued, but experience has shown that – while effective – they can be a costly emissions reduction policy. Finally, despite their large potential to generate environmental improvements, tax reforms outside of energy and vehicles, such as taxes on waste, plastic bags or chemicals, have been much less frequent.
- Finally, 2018 has seen the introduction of a few significant property tax reforms. Compared to previous years, characterised by limited reforms both in number and in scope, a few notable property tax reforms were introduced in 2018, including the doubling of the exemption threshold for the estate and gift tax in the United States, the introduction of a tax on securities accounts in Belgium, as well as France's repeal of the housing tax for 80% of households and the elimination of its net wealth tax which was replaced by a tax on real estate wealth.

The report is structured as follows: Chapter 1 gives an overview of the macroeconomic background; Chapter 2 presents the latest trends in tax revenues and tax mixes; and Chapter 3 gives an overview of the latest tax reform trends.

Notes

[1] The report includes all OECD countries as at 1 January 2018.

Chapter 1. Macroeconomic background

This chapter gives an overview of the main macroeconomic trends up until 2017. The purpose of this overview is to provide background information to help understand tax revenue trends as well as tax policy changes. Tax policy reforms are closely connected with economic trends: tax revenues are affected by changes in macroeconomic conditions and economic trends themselves are key drivers of tax reforms.

Macroeconomic trends

This chapter provides background information on macroeconomic conditions up until 2017 in order to help understand tax revenue trends and tax policy changes. It covers recent trends in growth, inflation, productivity, investment, the labour market, public finances and inequality. Tax policy developments are closely connected with economic trends: tax revenues are affected by changes in the macroeconomic conditions and these developments themselves are key drivers of tax reform.

Global growth picked up in 2017 and became increasingly broad-based

Global GDP growth is estimated to have been 3.7% in 2017, the fastest pace since 2011, albeit still below the longer-term average of around 4% seen in the two decades prior to the financial crisis (Figure 1.1). The long awaited lift to global growth, supported by policy stimulus, was accompanied by solid employment gains and an upturn in investment and global trade. Whilst welcome, the cyclical improvement in consumption and investment remained short of that achieved in past upswings (Figure 1.2). Per capita GDP growth improved in the majority of OECD economies in 2017, but shortfalls in the years after the crisis have yet to be overcome (OECD, 2018[1]). The lingering effects of prolonged sub-par growth after the financial crisis also continue to be reflected in subdued productivity and wage developments.

The global cyclical upturn became increasingly broad-based in 2017, with output growth picking up in both OECD and non-OECD countries (Figure 1.3). Amongst the advanced economies, fiscal and monetary support as well as the rebound in global trade helped to underpin growth in the euro area and Japan as well as in many other small open economies strongly connected to the major economies via value-chain linkages. Growth also rebounded in the United States, with accommodative monetary policy, strong asset prices gains and steady real income growth supporting domestic demand. OECD GDP growth picked up to 2.5%, around 0.7 percentage points higher than in the previous year. The rebound in global trade and strong policy-driven infrastructure investment in China contributed to the upturn in the EMEs, boosting external demand elsewhere, especially in Asia and in many commodity-exporting economies. Growth also picked up in India in the latter half of 2017, as the earlier drags from demonetisation and the introduction of the goods and services tax began to fade.

Figure 1.1. Real GDP growth

Year-on-year percentage changes

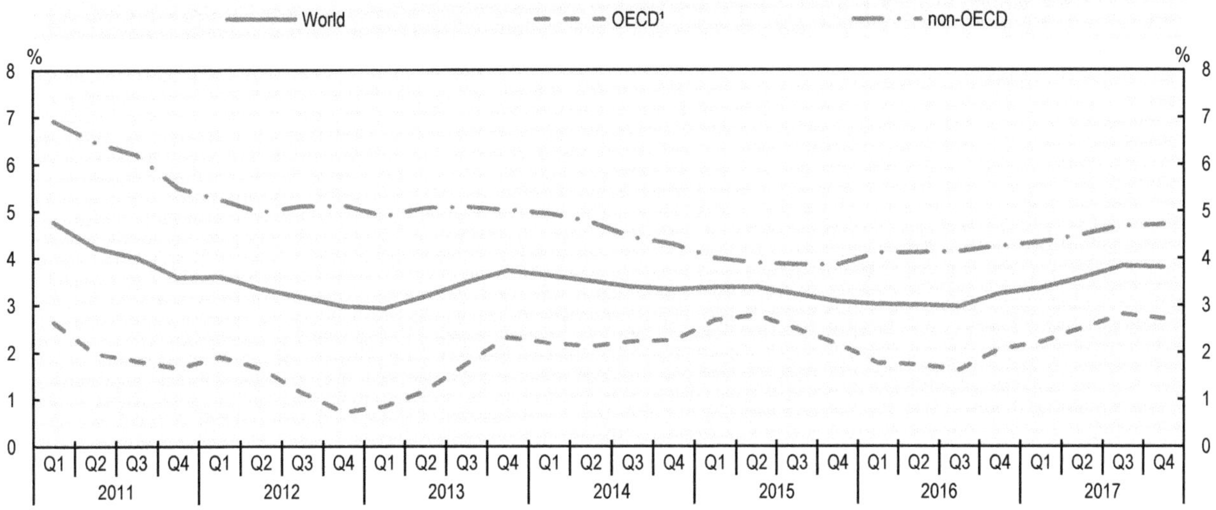

1. GDP measured using purchasing power parities.
2. With growth in Ireland computed using gross value added at constant prices excluding foreign-owned multinational enterprise dominated sectors.
Source: OECD Economic Outlook 103 database.

Figure 1.2. The recovery of consumption and investment in OECD countries

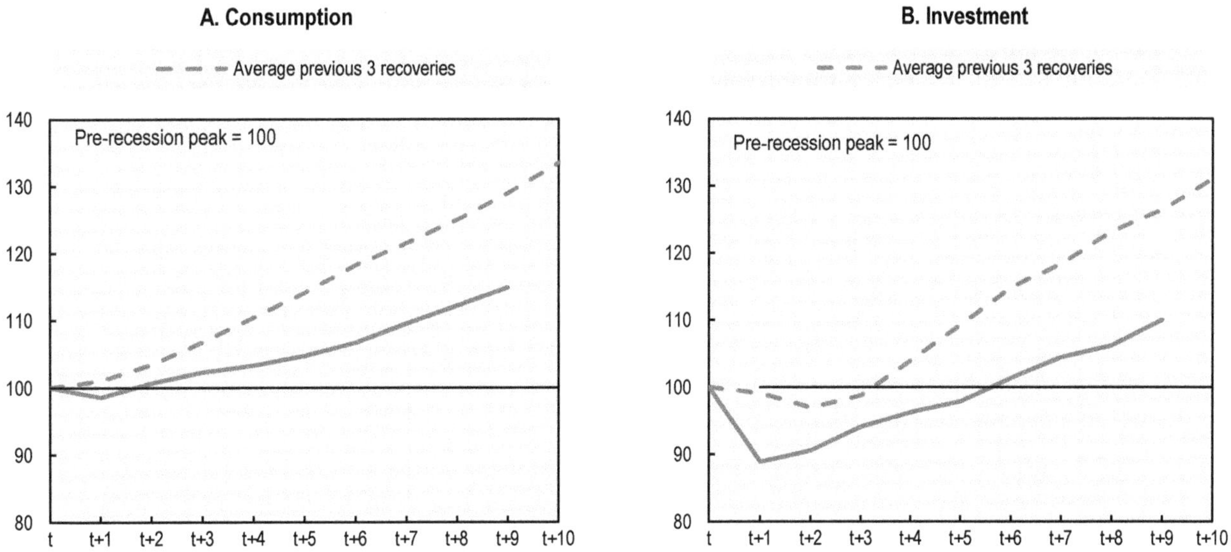

Note: Aggregate data for the OECD economies. Consumption is total consumers' expenditure and investment is total gross fixed capital formation. The average of the past three recoveries is an unweighted average of developments after 1973Q4, 1980Q1, 1990Q3 and 2008Q1. Series scaled to equal 100 in these quarters. All data are at constant prices.
Source: OECD Economic Outlook 103 database; and OECD calculations.

Figure 1.3. Real GDP growth in OECD countries

Percentage changes

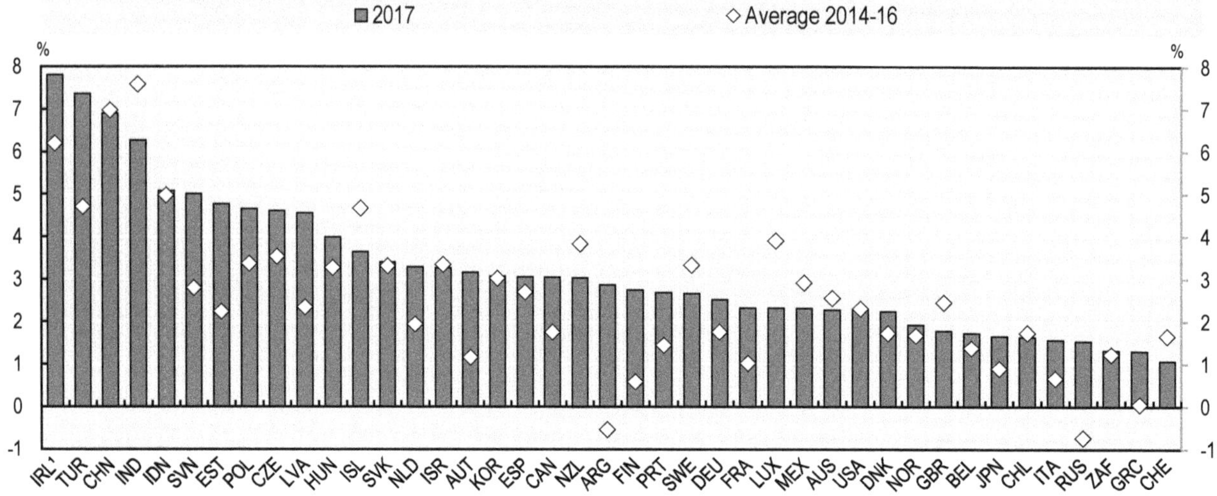

Note: With growth in Ireland computed using gross value added at constant prices excluding foreign-owned multinational enterprise dominated sectors.
Source: OECD Economic Outlook 103 database; and OECD calculations.

Labour market conditions continued to improve but the recovery in employment remained uneven

Labour market conditions continued to improve in 2017, with further declines in unemployment rates (Figure 1.4) and solid employment growth (Figure 1.5, Panel A). In the OECD as a whole, the harmonised unemployment rate fell to 5.5% by the end of 2017, marginally below the pre-crisis level. However, the level of unemployment remained elevated in some countries, particularly in some southern countries in the euro area (Figure 1.4). Long-term (over one year) and youth unemployment, and the number of involuntary part-time workers, still remained elevated. As of 2017, long-term unemployment represented 31% of total unemployment on average in the OECD economies (compared to under 25% in 2007), peaking at 73% in Greece and 59% in Italy. The large share of long-term unemployed people carries the risk of a rising number of discouraged workers - people who drop out of the labour force and experience skills attrition. Youth unemployment has declined from post-crisis peaks but still remains above pre-crisis levels in many OECD countries.

In most advanced economies, employment and labour participation rates are now above the level prior to the crisis, although the United States is a notable exception (OECD, 2017[2]) (OECD, 2018[1]). However, many OECD countries still have a high rate of involuntary part-time work compared with the pre-crisis level (OECD, 2017[3]). Wage growth generally remained subdued in the major economies, despite tighter labour markets (Figure 1.5, Panel B), in part reflecting weak productivity growth and low price inflation. However, some signs have emerged in early 2018 that wage pressures have begun to strengthen in several OECD economies (OECD, 2018[1]).

Figure 1.4. Unemployment rates in OECD countries

As a percentage of the labour force

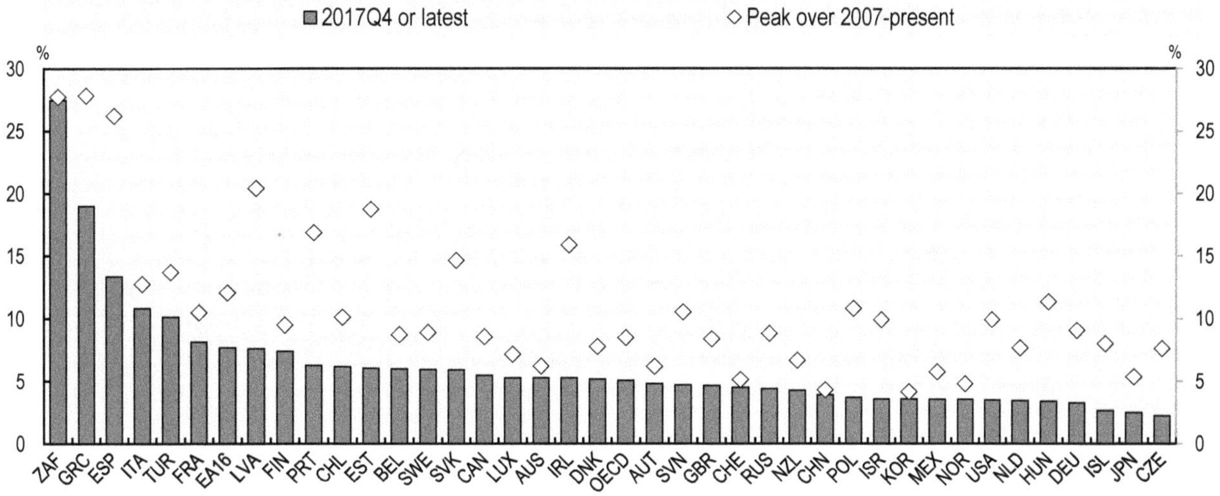

Source: OECD Economic Outlook 103 database; and OECD calculations.

Figure 1.5. Employment and real income growth

Year-on-year percentage changes

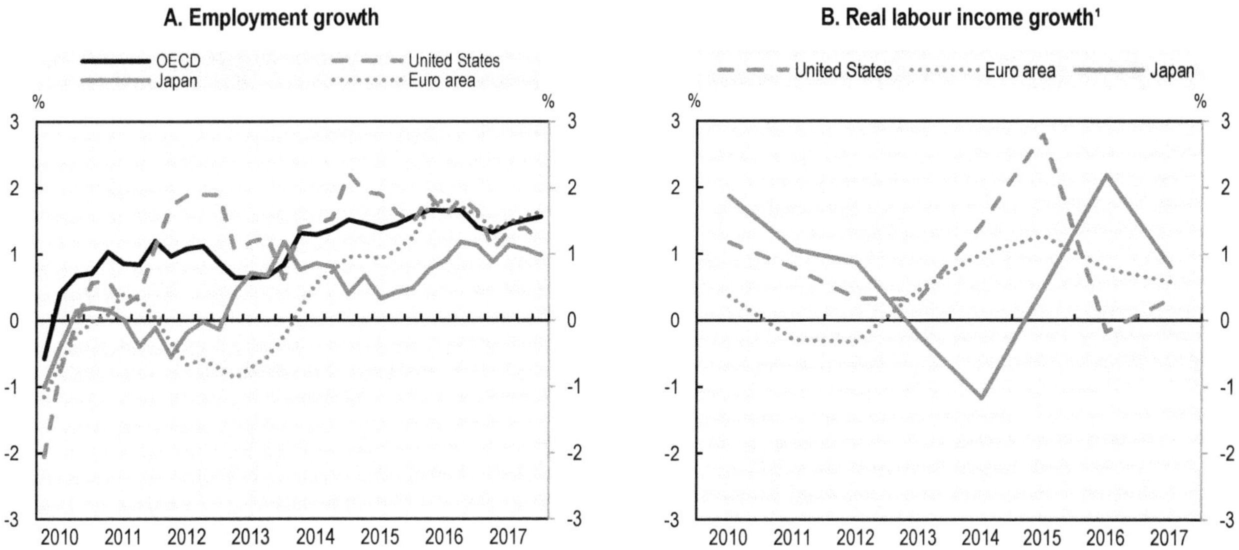

Note: Labour income per employee deflated by the private consumption deflator.
Source: OECD Economic Outlook 103 database; and OECD calculations.

Subdued wage growth has checked consumption growth and inflation

Private consumption growth remained broadly unchanged in the major economies and for the OECD area as a whole in 2017 (Figure 1.6, Panel B) in spite of the broader upturn in output growth. Cross-country differences in consumption growth since the crisis remain closely associated with differences in real income growth, especially labour incomes (OECD, 2016[4]). Although rising employment has supported household incomes, subdued real wage growth contributed to modest household income growth in 2017 in most advanced economies, which partly explains the moderate pace of consumption growth.

Headline inflation was pushed up during the course of 2017 by a significant rebound in commodity prices during the latter half of the year. This reduced household purchasing power, at least temporarily. However, underlying inflation (i.e. excluding food and energy) generally remained subdued in the major OECD economies and below official medium-term objectives. Oil prices were boosted by strong demand, and the extension of production restrictions in both OPEC and selected non-OPEC members until the end of 2018. In turn, higher prices helped to improve the growth outlook for commodity producers and the revenue raising capacity of governments in commodity-exporting economies. Metals prices were supported over the year by both temporary supply shortages in some producing countries and strong demand, especially from China. Commodity-importing economies faced rising import costs and input price inflation in the latter half of 2017.

Figure 1.6. Real private consumption expenditure growth and inflation

Year-on-year percentage changes

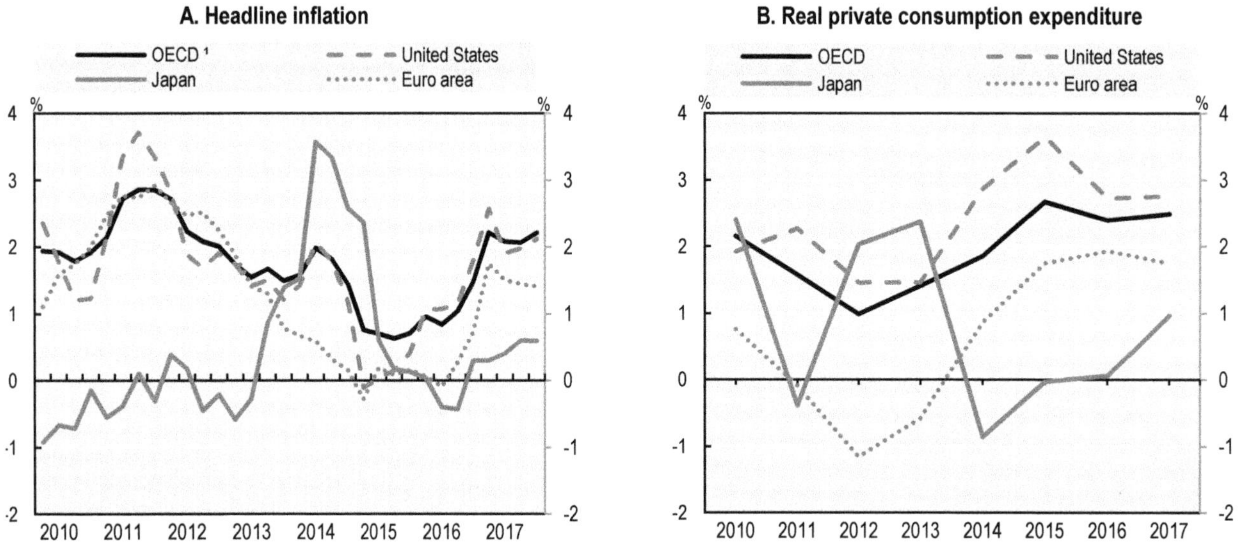

Note: OECD aggregate is computed based on different indicators: United States: price index for personal consumption expenditure; euro area members and United Kingdom: harmonised index of consumer prices; and other countries: national consumer price index.
Source: OECD Economic Outlook 103 database; and OECD calculations.

Stronger investment growth is now supporting the broad-based recovery, but productivity growth remains low

After having been subdued for a long period, fixed capital investment recovered in 2017, with the private investment growth rate outpacing its average since 2010 in many OECD economies (Figure 1.7). Total investment in the advanced economies rose by 3.6%, with business investment rising by 4½% (from under 2½% in 2016). Nonetheless, the investment upturn remained weaker than necessary to help bring growth of the productive capital stock back to pre-crisis norms, limiting prospects for productivity growth (OECD,

2017[2]). Factors holding back investment include diminished long-term growth expectations, a lack of business dynamism in some economies and uncertainty (OECD, 2018[1]). Resources trapped in unproductive firms (Andrews, Criscuolo and Gal, 2016[5]), and a slowdown of new reforms aiming to improve product market competition (OECD, 2018[6]) have also damped incentives to invest. Nonetheless, the recent upturn in investment suggests that some of these constraints may have begun to ease.

Global foreign direct investment (FDI) inflows declined by 18% in 2017 (OECD, 2018[7]). FDI inflows fell by over one-third in the OECD countries, largely reflecting lower inflows into the United Kingdom and the United States (two of the main host economies for inward FDI), but rose slightly in the non-OECD G20 economies. Despite the lower level of new inflows, the aggregate stock of inward FDI in the OECD economies rose further in 2017, to over 40% of GDP, representing over three-fifths of the estimated global inward FDI stock.

In spite of stronger output growth in 2017, labour productivity growth remained sluggish, reflecting slow growth in productive capital per worker and in the diffusion of new ideas and technology embodied in new equipment. Labour productivity growth in OECD countries since the crisis has generally fallen significantly below that seen in the decade prior to the crisis, checking future potential growth (Figure 1.8). Moreover, in the post-crisis period, there has been relatively weak growth in multi-factor productivity, which reflects the efficiency with which inputs are used (OECD, 2015[8]). Productivity gaps between firms have widened as frontier firms have continued to make gains but laggard firms have under-performed, contributing to rising inequality (Andrews, Criscuolo and Gal, 2016[5]). These trends have led to low income growth for many households, particularly at the bottom of the income distribution, which has in turn held back aggregate consumption growth.

Figure 1.7. Gross fixed capital formation growth in OECD countries

Percentage changes

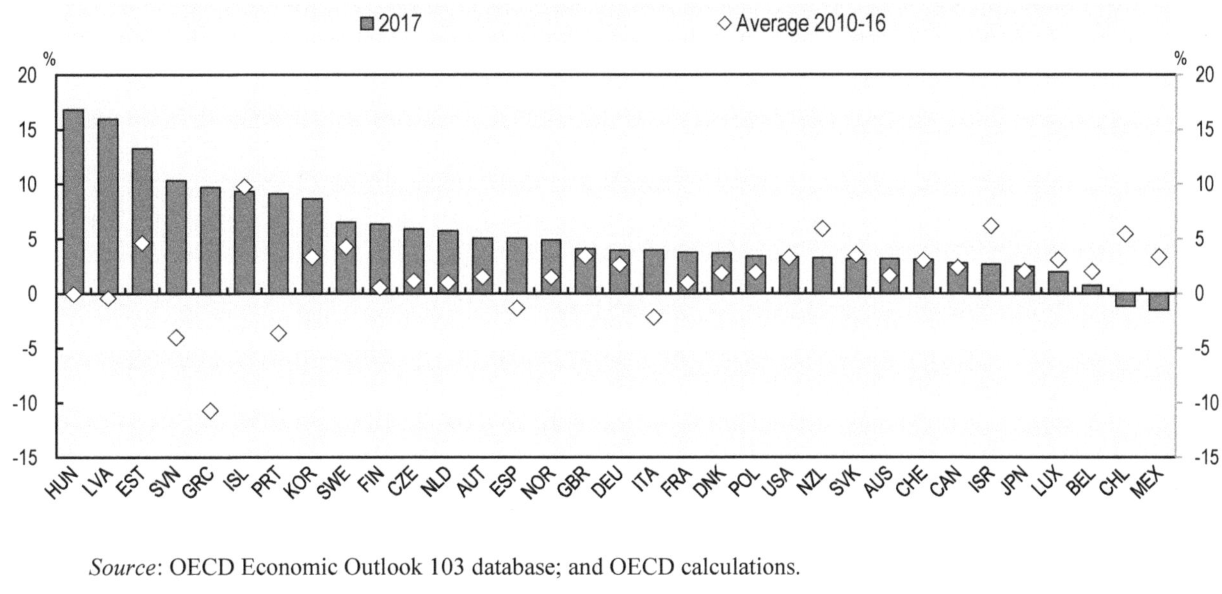

Source: OECD Economic Outlook 103 database; and OECD calculations.

Figure 1.8. Labour productivity in OECD countries since the crisis

Percentage changes

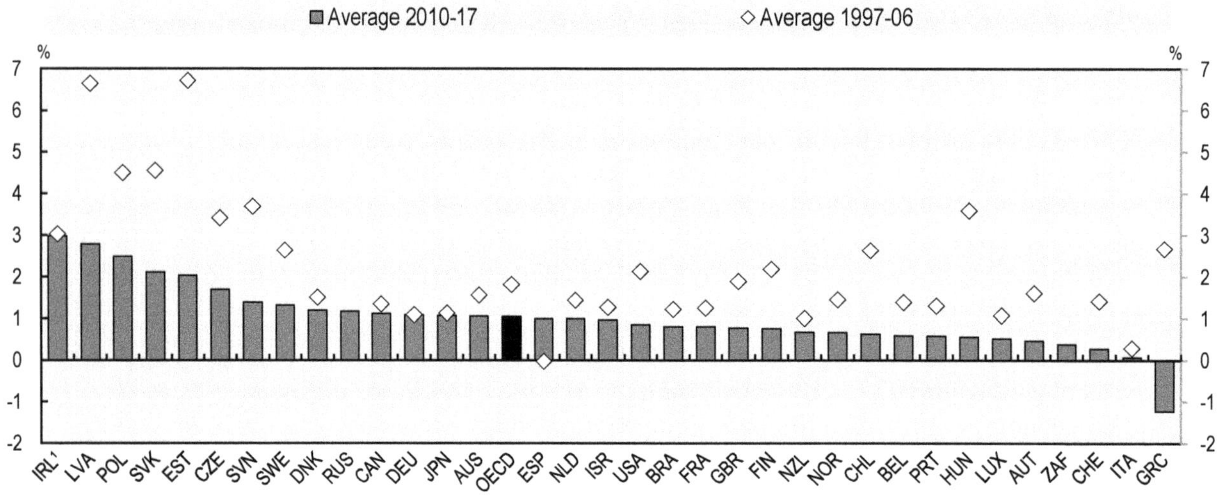

Note: With growth in Ireland computed using gross value added at constant prices excluding foreign-owned multinational enterprise dominated sectors.

Source: OECD Economic Outlook 103 database; and OECD calculations.

Budget balances have improved and public debt ratios have stabilised or fallen in many countries

After rising rapidly in the aftermath of the financial crisis, general government gross debt as a share of GDP has stabilised in the OECD area at a high level. The aggregate OECD gross debt-to-GDP ratio stood at about 111% in 2017, up from 97% in 2010 (Figure 1.9, Panel A). The debt to GDP ratio has declined in the euro area over the past three years, but much of this is accounted for by a sharp decline in Germany. Across the OECD, there were wide differences between countries in 2017, with gross general government financial liabilities ranging from 13% of GDP in Estonia to 224% in Japan.

The overall budget balance as a share of GDP improved further in the majority of OECD countries in 2017 (Figure 1.9, Panel B). For the OECD countries as a whole, the budget deficit dropped to 2% of GDP in 2017 from 8.5% at the height of the crisis in 2009. There was a wide difference between OECD countries in 2017, with general government budget surpluses in Germany and Korea (between 1-3% of GDP) and sizeable deficits in the United States and Japan (around 3½% of GDP). Stronger nominal growth and lower unemployment have contributed to the improvement in fiscal positions in recent years, adding to the effects from past fiscal consolidation. The overall fiscal stance, reflected in the year-on-year change in the underlying primary balance[1], became mildly expansionary in 2017, by about 0.1% of GDP in the median OECD economy. Further expansionary fiscal measures are being implemented in the majority of OECD countries in 2018-19 (OECD, 2018[11]), particularly the United States.

Figure 1.9. General government gross debt and budget balance

As a percentage of GDP

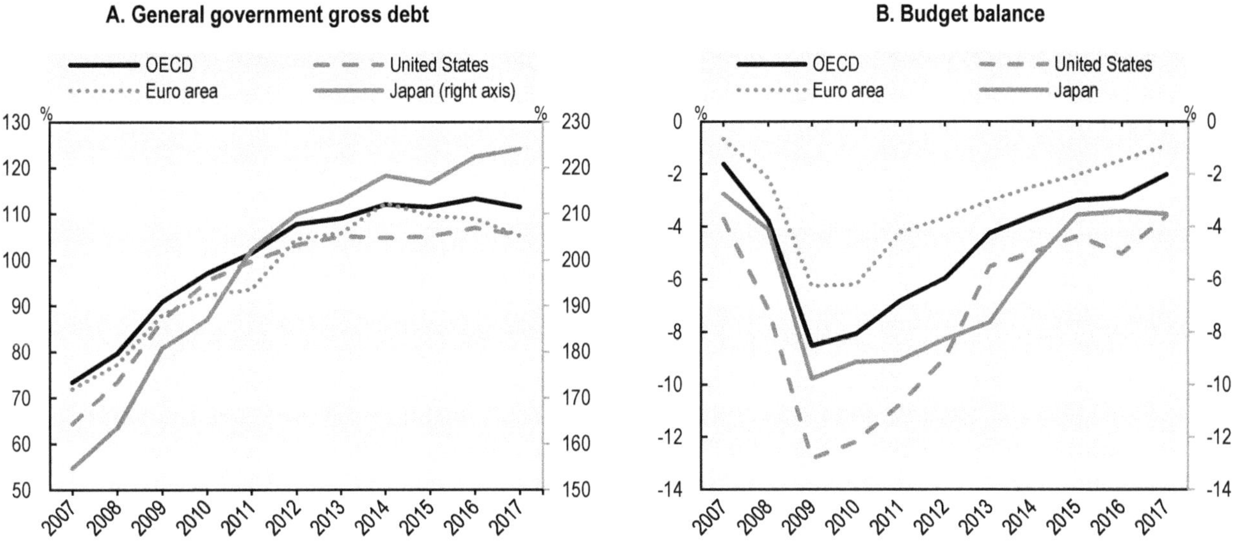

Source: OECD Economic Outlook 103 database; and OECD calculations.

Government bond yields have remained very low by historical standards in many OECD countries, despite a gentle upturn from mid-2016, reflecting expectations of continued accommodative monetary policy for some time and low term premia. Thus, a significant share of outstanding government debt was still trading at negative yields in 2017. As shown in Figure 1.10, gross government interest payments as a share of GDP generally remained below levels seen following the crisis in OECD countries, despite higher debt levels, increasing fiscal space in many countries.

Figure 1.10. Gross government interest payments in OECD countries

As a percentage of GDP

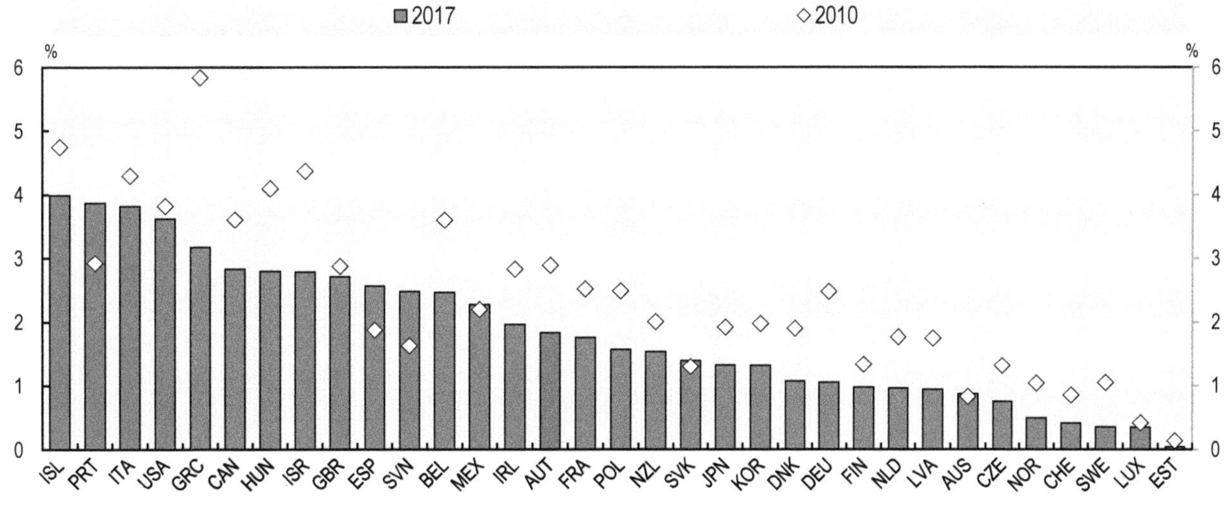

Source: OECD Economic Outlook 103 database; and OECD calculations.

Income inequality remains high in many OECD countries

Inequality in many OECD countries remains high by historical standards. High income inequality compounds the drag on economy-wide household spending from weak income growth, as the higher-income households in which income growth has been concentrated typically have a lower marginal propensity to consume. While cross-country patterns of income inequality depend to some extent on how inequality is measured, the most widely used measure is the Gini coefficient (OECD, 2017[9]). On this basis, inequality of market incomes (before taxes and transfers) has remained broadly stable since the financial crisis on average in OECD countries, but the extent of the change in market income inequality since 2010 has varied widely across countries (Figure 1.11).

On average in OECD countries, taxes and transfers reduce income inequality by slightly over a quarter; over two-thirds of this reduction is due to transfers and the remaining portion due to taxes (Causa and Hermansen, 2017[10]). There are considerable differences amongst countries, with the highest redistribution in Finland and the weakest in Mexico. The impact of redistribution is even higher if non-cash transfers from governments, such as education and healthcare, are taken into account (OECD, 2016[11]). After taking into account redistributive policies, around half of the 33 countries for which data are available reported an increase in disposable income inequality between 2011 and 2015 (Figure 1.12). The extent of redistribution via taxes and transfers has declined in many OECD countries since 2010, in part reflecting the upturn in the business cycle and declining unemployment. Other contributing factors may include some reduction in transfers as part of fiscal consolidation and reduced progressivity of the tax system.

At the aggregate OECD level, the pace of disposable household income growth has also differed across different parts of the income distribution in recent years. The incomes of those in the top 10% of the distribution have risen faster than average (median) incomes and those at the bottom end of the income distribution (Figure 1.13). Thus, many households have seen little growth in real disposable incomes over the past decade. In around half of the major emerging market economies, disposable income inequality has decreased since the mid-2000s, including in Brazil, Turkey, South Africa and China (OECD, 2017[9]) (OECD, 2017[12]). However, it has increased in India and Russia.

Figure 1.11. Market income, post-transfer and disposable income Gini coefficients

2015 or latest, for total population

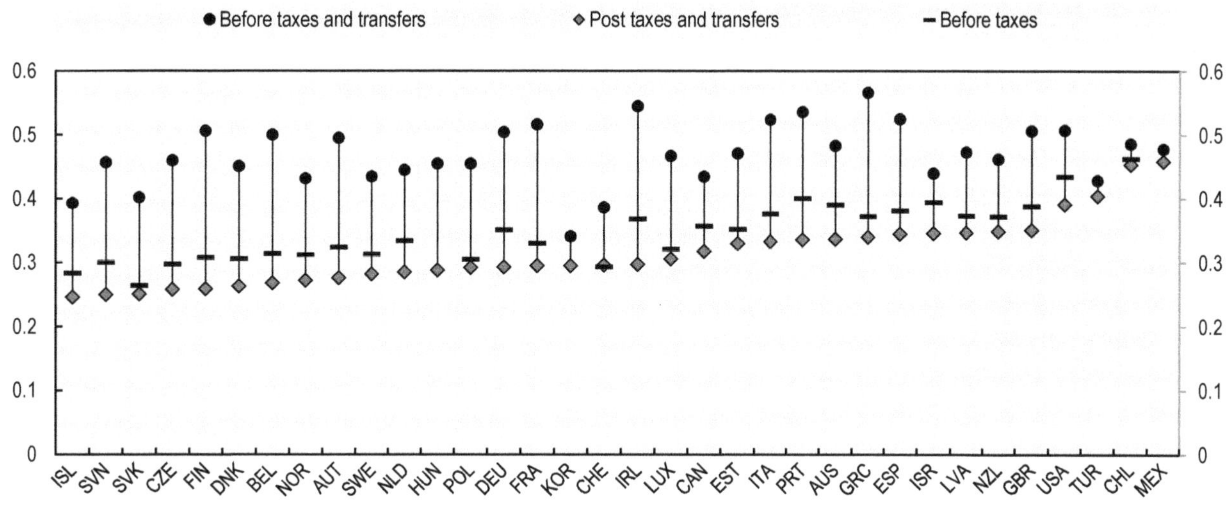

Source: OECD Income Distribution Database (IDD).

Figure 1.12. Disposable income Gini coefficients

Total population

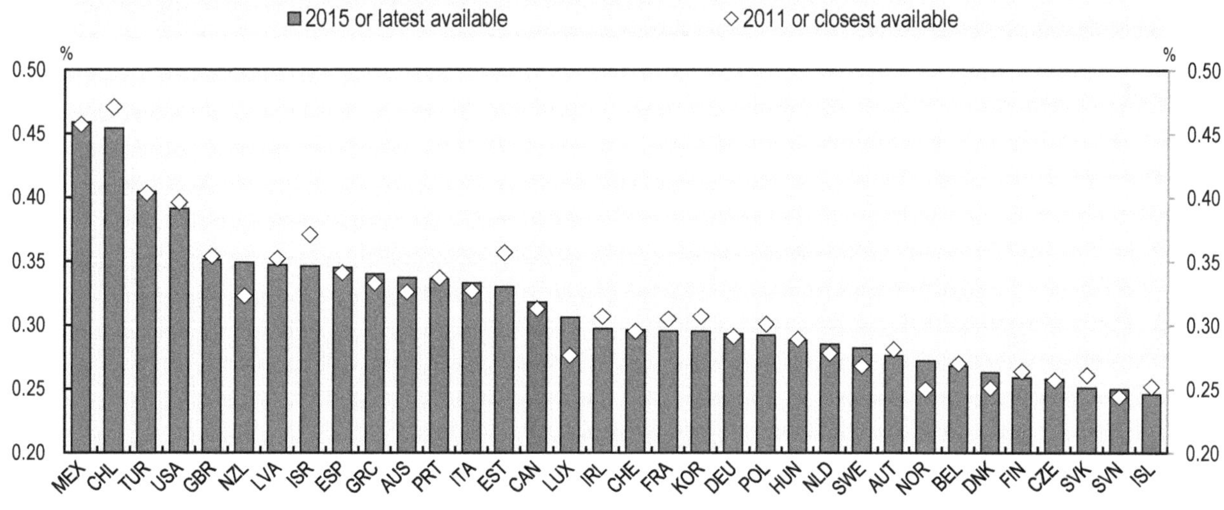

Source: OECD income Distribution Database (IDD).

Figure 1.13. Household real disposable income growth

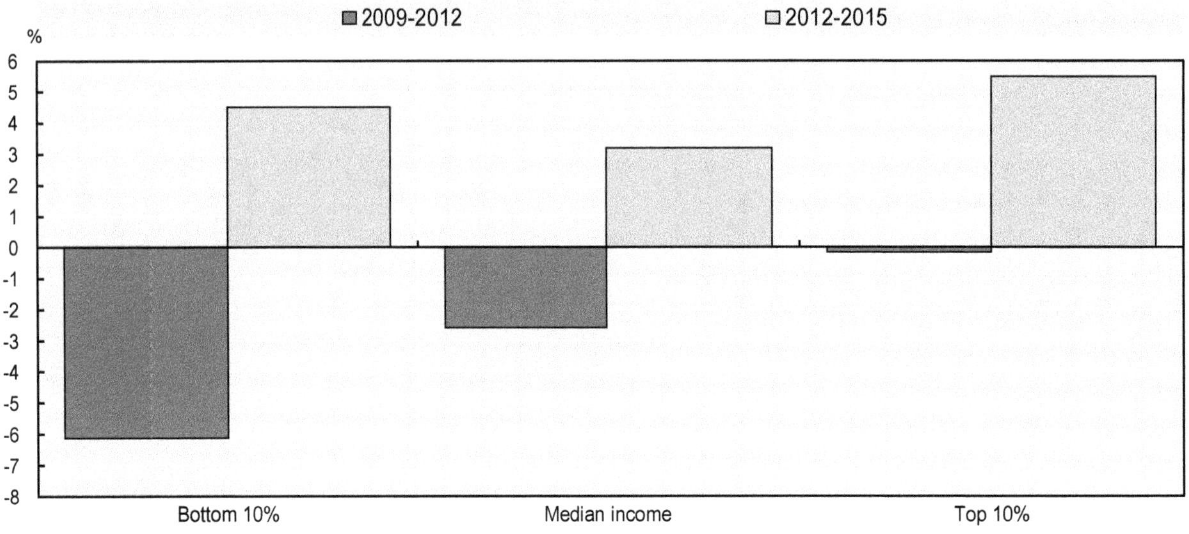

Note: The income series are averages of 17 OECD countries.
Source: OECD Income Distribution database (IDD); and OECD calculations.

Notes

[1] The underlying primary balance is the fiscal balance excluding net interest payments and adjusted for the economic cycle and for budgetary one-offs.

References

Andrews, D., C. Criscuolo and P. Gal (2016), "The Global Productivity Slowdown, Technology Divergence and Public Policy: A Firm Level Perspective", *The Future of Productivity: Main Background Papers*. [5]

Causa, O. and M. Hermansen (2017), "Income redistribution through taxes and transfers across OECD countries", *OECD Economics Department Working Papers*, No. 1453, OECD Publishing, Paris, http://dx.doi.org/10.1787/bc7569c6-en. [10]

OECD (2018), *Economic Policy Reforms 2018: Going for Growth Interim Report*, OECD Publishing, Paris, http://dx.doi.org/10.1787/growth-2018-en. [6]

OECD (2018), *FDI in Figures*, http://www.oecd.org/daf/inv/investment-policy/FDI-in-Figures-April-2018.pdf. [7]

OECD (2018), *OECD Economic Outlook, Volume 2018 Issue 1*, OECD Publishing, Paris, http://dx.doi.org/10.1787/eco_outlook-v2018-1-en. [1]

OECD (2017), *Economic Policy Reforms 2017: Going for Growth*, OECD Publishing, Paris, http://dx.doi.org/10.1787/growth-2017-en. [9]

OECD (2017), *OECD Economic Outlook, Volume 2017 Issue 2*, OECD Publishing, Paris, http://dx.doi.org/10.1787/eco_outlook-v2017-2-en. [2]

OECD (2017), *OECD Economic Surveys: China 2017*, OECD Publishing, Paris, http://dx.doi.org/10.1787/eco_surveys-chn-2017-en. [12]

OECD (2017), *OECD Employment Outlook 2017*, OECD Publishing, Paris, http://dx.doi.org/10.1787/empl_outlook-2017-en. [3]

OECD (2016), *Inequality Update - November 2016*, http://dx.doi.org/www.oecd.org/social/OECD2016-Income-Inequality-Update.pdf. [11]

OECD (2016), *OECD Economic Outlook, Volume 2016 Issue 2*, OECD Publishing, Paris, http://dx.doi.org/10.1787/eco_outlook-v2016-2-en. [4]

OECD (2015), *The Future of Productivity*, OECD Publishing, Paris, http://dx.doi.org/10.1787/9789264248533-en. [8]

Chapter 2. Tax revenue trends

This chapter describes tax revenue trends – looking at both total tax-to-GDP ratios and tax mixes – in OECD countries, Argentina, Indonesia and South Africa. The analysis covers tax revenue trends until 2016, the latest year for which comparable tax revenue data is available. This overview of tax revenue trends is useful to understand the effects of past tax policy reforms and sets the stage for the subsequent discussion on the tax reforms that were recently introduce

Trends in tax revenues

This chapter describes the latest tax revenue trends – looking at both total tax-to-GDP ratios and tax mixes – in all 35 OECD countries[1] as well as in Argentina, Indonesia and South Africa. The analysis covers tax revenue trends until 2016, the latest year for which comparable tax revenue data is available (OECD, 2017[1]). This overview of tax revenue trends is useful to understand the effects of past tax policy reforms and provides background to the subsequent discussion on countries' latest tax reforms (Chapter 3).

Overall, this chapter shows that tax revenues across countries have on average continued to increase. A majority of countries recorded increases in their tax revenues as a share of GDP between 2015 and 2016. However, 14 out of the 34 countries for which 2016 data[2] is available experienced decreases in their tax-to-GDP ratios. Compared to the 2014-2015 period, the number of countries recording tax revenue falls increased but the magnitude of these revenue falls was smaller. The chapter also highlights that while there has been an increase in average tax-to-GDP ratios, tax revenues generally account for a lower share of government expenditure than before the crisis. Regarding the composition of tax revenues, countries are on average collecting an increasing share of their revenues from personal income taxes, partly reflecting the effects of recent tax reforms.

Tax revenues vary significantly across countries

Tax revenues as a share of GDP vary significantly across countries. In 2016, Denmark had the highest tax revenues as a percentage of GDP (i.e. tax-to-GDP ratio) among all the countries covered in the report, reaching 45.9%, closely followed by France (45.3%). Seven countries recorded tax-to-GDP ratios above 40% and 20 countries had tax revenues between 30% and 40% of GDP. The country with the lowest tax-to-GDP ratio was Indonesia, with total tax revenues amounting to only 11.8% of its GDP. The second and third lowest tax-to-GDP ratios were recorded by Mexico (17.2%) and Chile (20.4%) (Figure 2.1).

Figure 2.1. Tax-to-GDP ratios by country in 2016

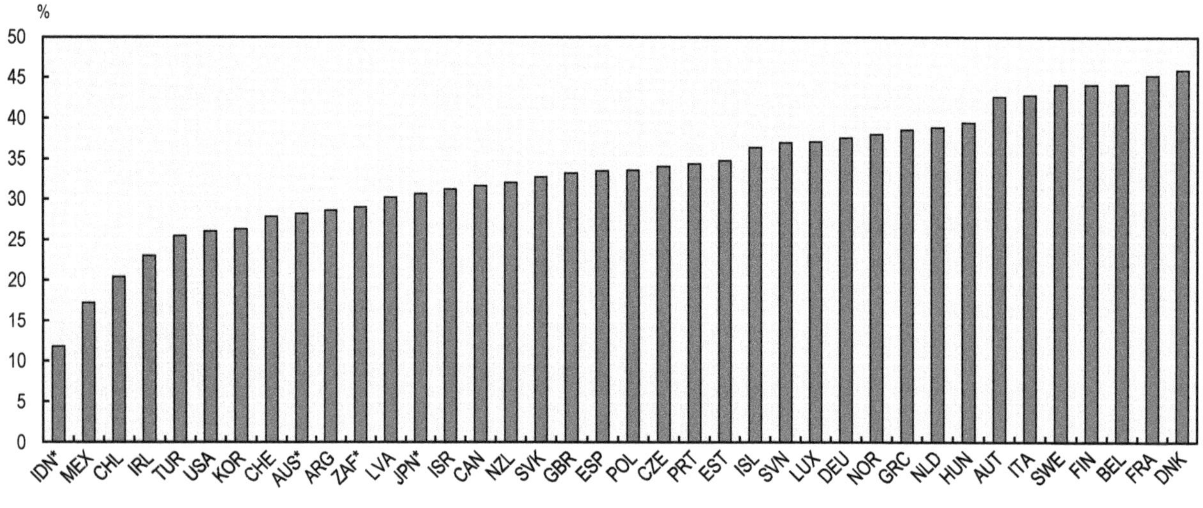

Note: 2015 data used for Australia, Indonesia, Japan and South Africa.
Source: OECD and Global Revenue Statistics databases.

There is a positive correlation between countries' tax-to-GDP ratios and GDP per capita levels. Countries with lower GDP per capita tend to have lower tax revenues as a share of GDP (e.g. Argentina, Chile, Indonesia, Mexico, South Africa and Turkey), while high-GDP per capita countries tend to have higher tax-to-GDP ratios (e.g. Scandinavian countries, Austria, Belgium, France). However, as shown in Figure 2.2, there are many exceptions, particularly at the higher GDP per capita levels with some countries characterised by high levels of GDP per capita but comparatively low tax-to-GDP ratios (e.g. Anglo-Saxon countries, Korea, Japan). There are also countries with below-average levels of GDP per capita but relatively high tax revenues as a share of GDP (e.g. some Central and Southern European countries). Figure 2.2 also highlights that levels of tax-to-GDP ratios also follow regional patterns.

Figure 2.2. Tax revenues as a share of GDP and GDP per capita

GDP per capita in current USD ppp (x axis) and tax-to-GDP ratios in % (y axis)

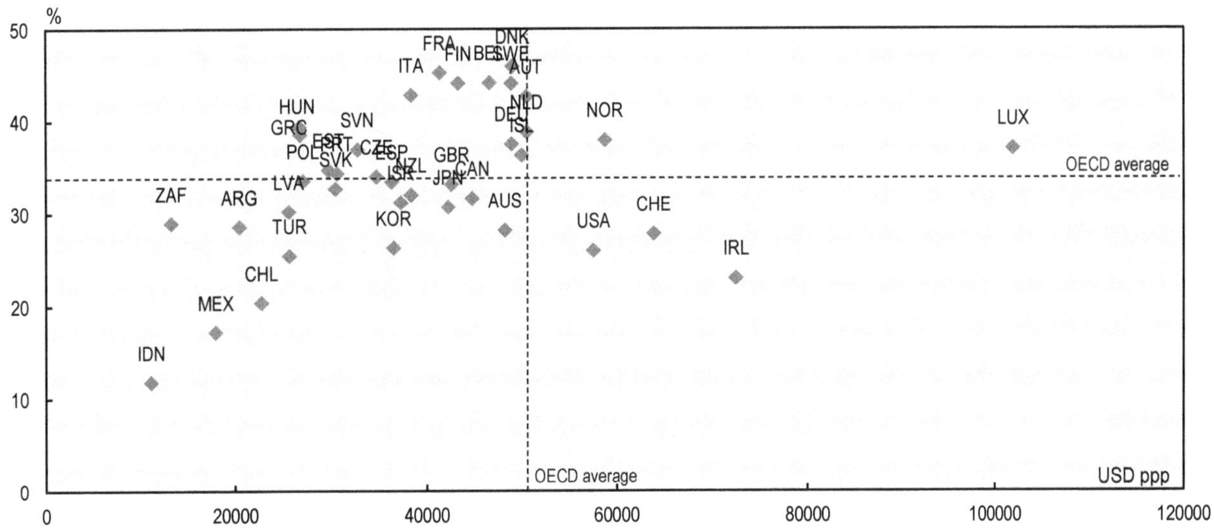

Source: OECD and Global Revenue Statistics databases and Aggregate National Accounts.

The OECD average tax-to-GDP ratio reached a new record level in 2016

In 2016, the OECD average tax-to-GDP ratio reached a new record level. Between 2015 and 2016, the OECD average tax-to-GDP ratio increased from 34.0% to 34.3%. This is the seventh consecutive annual increase since the low-point experienced in many countries in 2008 and 2009 as a consequence of the financial and economic crisis (Figure 2.3). Looking at longer-term trends, the 2016 OECD average tax-to-GDP ratio was the highest ever recorded since the OECD started collecting tax revenue data in 1965, with a total increase of close to 10 percentage points over the last 50 years (Figure 2.4).

Increasing tax-to-GDP ratios have been a common trend across different groups of countries. In addition to the OECD average tax-to-GDP ratio, Figure 2.3 shows average tax-to-GDP ratios for the 14 countries covered in the report that are members of the G20 (referred to as G14 countries) and for the 21 countries that are EU members. The three groups of countries have experienced increases in their tax-to-GDP ratios since the crisis. Figure 2.3 also shows that the gaps between the G14, the OECD and the OECD EU average tax-to-GDP ratios have narrowed since 1990, suggesting a degree of convergence in tax-to-GDP ratios.

Figure 2.3. Tax-to-GDP ratios in different groups of countries

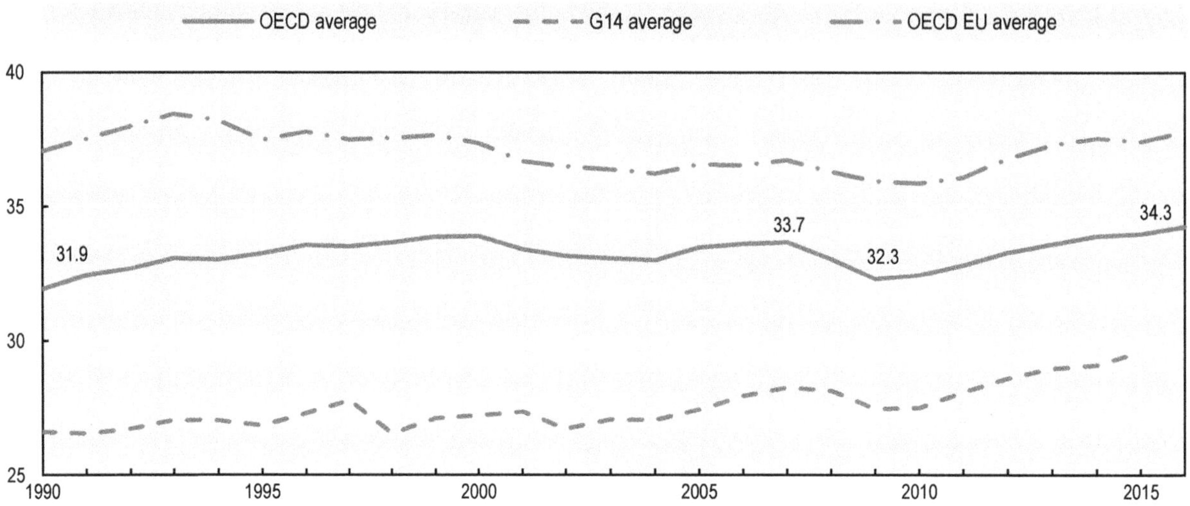

Note: G14 countries refer to the 14 countries covered in this report that are members of the G20 including Argentina, Australia, Canada, France, Germany, Indonesia, Italy, Japan, Mexico, Korea, South Africa, Turkey, the United Kingdom and the United States. The OECD EU average is the average for the 21 OECD countries that are members of the European Union.
Source: OECD and Global Revenue Statistics databases.

Figure 2.4. Long-term evolution of the OECD average tax-to-GDP ratio

Average and range of tax-to-GDP ratios in the OECD, 1965 – 2016

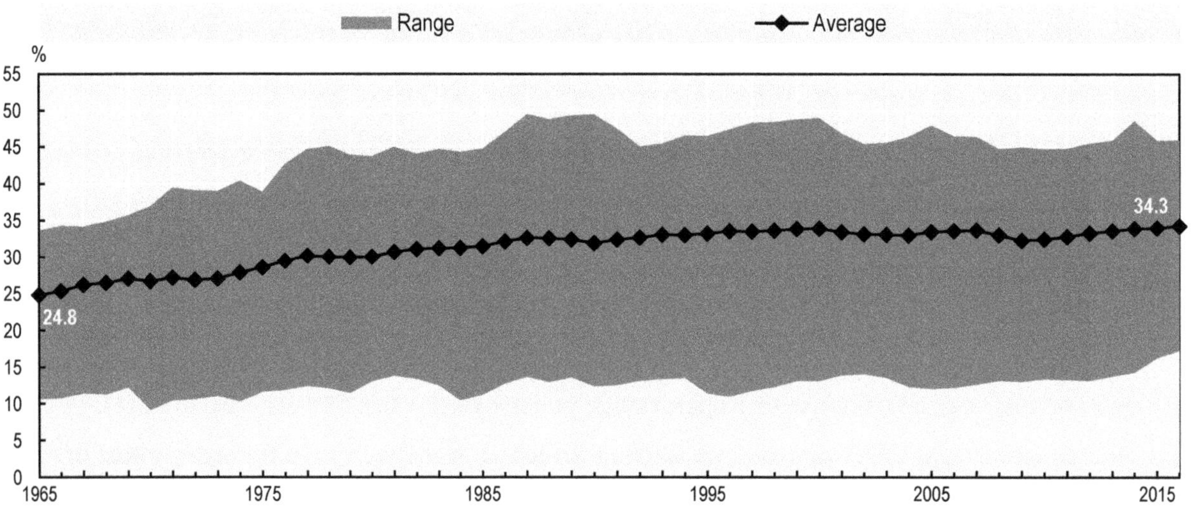

Source: OECD Revenue Statistics database.

The rise in tax revenues across OECD countries in the years following the crisis was partly the result of active fiscal consolidation measures. In addition to economic fluctuations, which have effects on tax bases through changes in levels of investment, employment and sales of goods and services, tax revenues are affected by changes in tax policy. In the years that followed the crisis, the adoption of tax reforms aimed at strengthening public finances was one of the factors accounting for the increase in tax revenues. More recently, however, the focus of tax policies has shifted away from fiscal consolidation towards supporting businesses and households through tax cuts (OECD, 2017[1]) (OECD, 2017[2]). The effects of these tax cuts on future tax revenues are unclear. While they could put a halt to the trend of increasing tax revenues as a share of GDP, increased levels of profitability and higher labour market participation rates may have the opposite effect.

Tax revenue trends have differed across countries

A majority of countries experienced an increase in their tax-to-GDP ratios between 2015 and 2016 (OECD, 2016[3]). Indeed, 20 of the 34 countries for which 2016 data is available recorded an increase in their tax revenues as a share of GDP (Figure 2.5). In all these countries, the increase was due to tax revenues increasing more than GDP (Figure 2.6). The tax-to-GDP ratio increase was largest in Greece, due to higher revenues from taxes on income and taxes on goods and services (Figure 2.5), which were partly the consequence of tax increases aimed at enhancing the country's fiscal sustainability (OECD, 2016[3]). Tax-to-GDP ratio increases above one percentage point were also recorded in the Netherlands, Latvia, Korea and Poland.

Figure 2.5. Percentage point changes in tax-to-GDP ratios by country between 2015 and 2016

Percentage point changes in tax-to-GDP ratios decomposed by type of tax

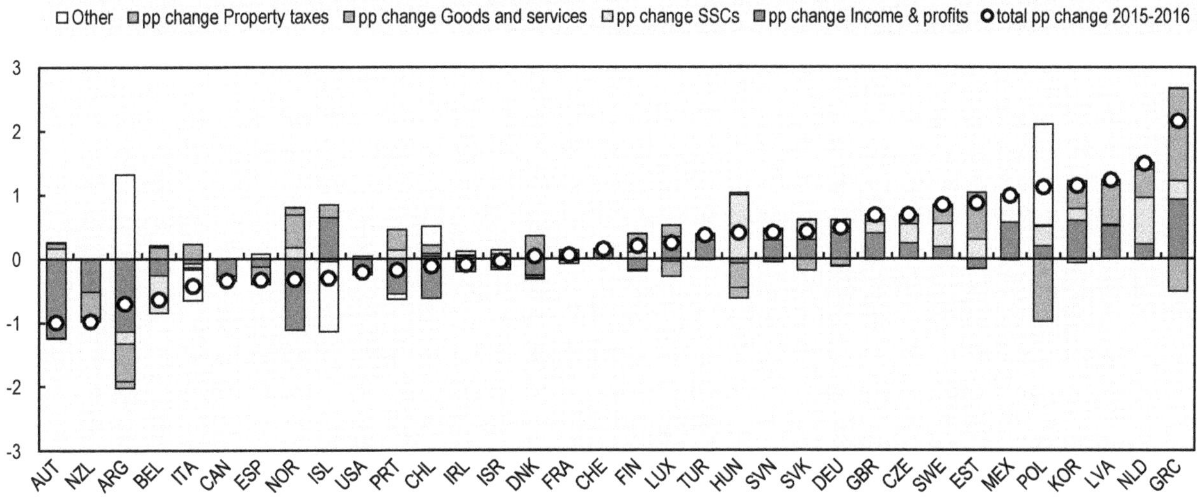

Note: No data for Australia, Indonesia, Japan and South Africa.
Source: OECD and Global Revenue Statistics databases.

On the other hand, 14 countries experienced a decrease in their tax-to-GDP ratios in 2016 relative to 2015. This number is an increase compared to the 2014-2015 period, when only seven countries experienced a decrease in their tax-to-GDP ratios. However, the revenue falls were smaller than the ones reported between 2014 and 2015, with no decreases exceeding one percentage point between 2015 and 2016 (Figure 2.5). The largest decreases were recorded by Austria and New Zealand, due to a decrease in taxes on income and profits as a share of GDP as well as a decrease in taxes on goods and services as a share of GDP for New Zealand. Tax-to-GDP ratio declines were also seen in Argentina, Belgium, Canada, Chile, Iceland, Ireland, Israel, Italy, Norway, Portugal, Spain and the United States. In all countries but Norway, the falls were due to nominal tax revenues increasing less than nominal GDP, whereas in Norway, both tax revenues and GDP fell (Figure 2.6).

Figure 2.6. Changes in nominal tax revenues and nominal GDP between 2015 and 2016

Relative changes in %

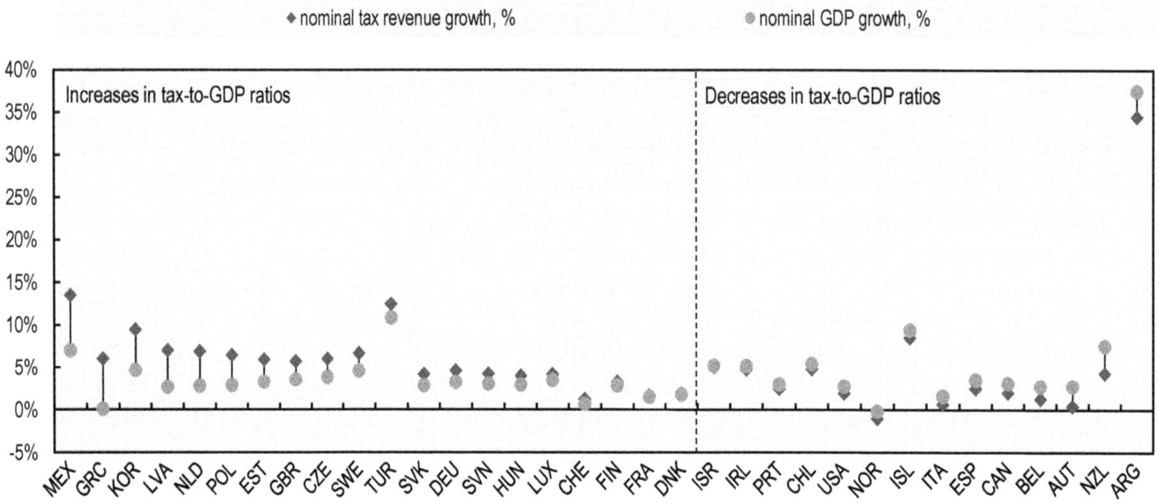

Note: No data for Australia, Indonesia, Japan and South Africa.
Source: OECD and Global Revenue Statistics databases.

Looking at tax revenue changes between 2007 and 2016 also shows differing trends across countries. 21 out of the 38 countries covered in this report experienced an increase in their tax revenues as a share of GDP compared to pre-crisis levels (Figure 2.7). The largest tax-to-GDP ratio increase between 2007 and 2016 was recorded by Greece (7.4 percentage points). Four other countries – Argentina, Mexico, the Slovak Republic and Estonia – experienced increases of at least 3 percentage points. However, 17 out of 38 countries had lower tax-to-GDP ratios in 2016 than in 2007. Ireland experienced the biggest fall, from 30.4% to 23.0%, mainly because of exceptional GDP growth in 2015. The second largest fall was recorded in Norway, from 42.1% of GDP in 2007 to 38.0% in 2016, largely due to a decline in earnings in the oil sector which in turn caused a sharp drop in corporate income tax revenues.

Figure 2.7. Percentage point changes in tax-to-GDP ratios by country between 2007 and 2016

Percentage point changes in tax-to-GDP ratios decomposed by type of tax

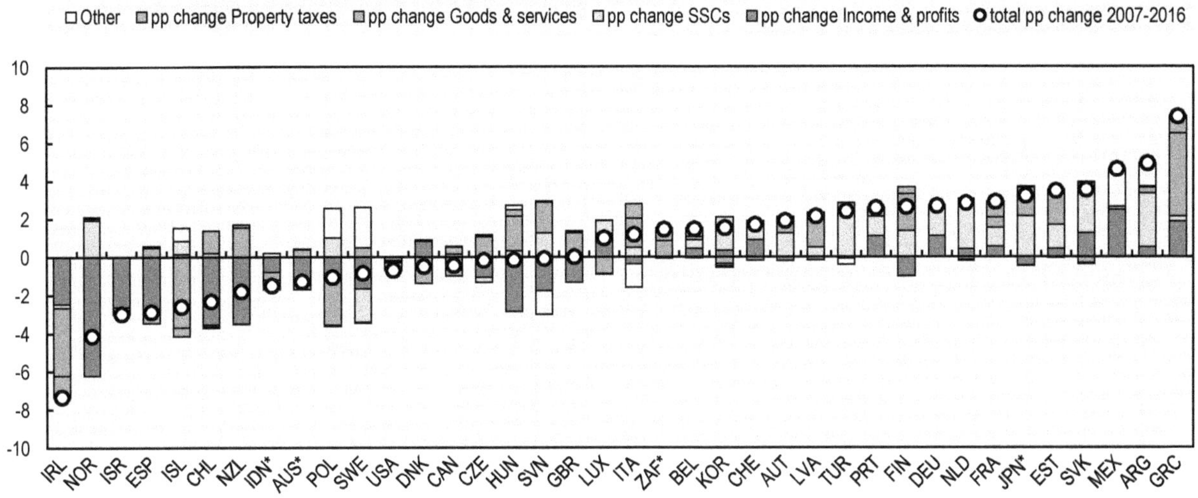

Note: P.p. changes between 2007 and 2015 used for Australia, Indonesia, Japan and South Africa.
Source: OECD and Global Revenue Statistics databases.

Larger public debts and lower tax-to-GDP ratios before the crisis were often associated with greater increases in tax-to-GDP ratios in the years following the crisis. Generally, countries with high levels of public debt in 2007 experienced greater increases in their tax-to-GDP ratios although there were exceptions (Figure 2.8, right panel). There is also a negative correlation between total tax revenues as a share of GDP in 2007 and percentage point changes in tax-to-GDP ratios between 2007 and 2015, suggesting a convergence trend in tax-to-GDP ratios across countries (Figure 2.7, left panel). However, more work is needed to understand convergence patterns in tax-to-GDP ratios across countries.

Figure 2.8. Percentage point changes in tax-to-GDP ratios between 2007 and 2016, tax revenues and levels of public debt in 2007

P.p. changes in tax-to-GDP ratios between 2007 and 2016 and tax-to-GDP ratios in 2007 (left panel) and p.p. changes in tax-to-GDP ratios between 2007 and 2016 and public debt as a % of GDP in 2007 (right panel)

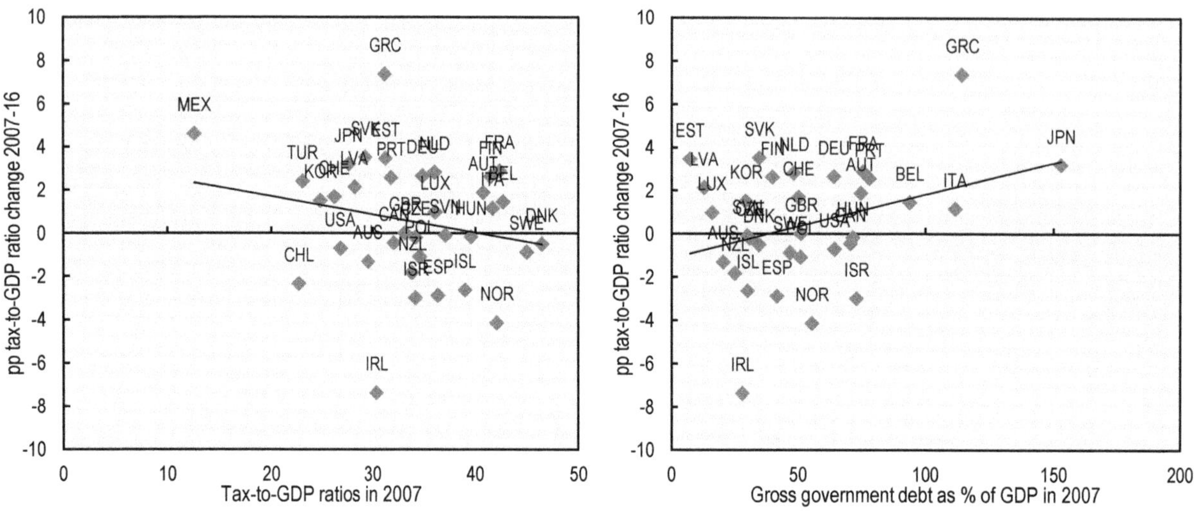

Note: P.p. changes in tax-to-GDP ratios between 2007 and 2015 used for Australia and Japan. No data for Argentina, Chile, Indonesia, Mexico, South Africa and Turkey.
Source: OECD Economic Outlook 102 database and OECD Revenue Statistics database.

Recent trends in tax revenues – along with declining public expenditure – have contributed to improvements in public finances

The financial and economic crisis led simultaneously to a drop in tax revenues and a significant increase in public expenditure in OECD countries on average. Consequently, a bigger part of total government expenditure had to be financed by either non-tax revenues or debt. As shown in Figure 2.9 (left panel), while tax revenues covered on average 84.5% of government expenditure in 2000 in the OECD, they dropped to only around 70% of public expenditure in 2009. The remaining 30% of public expenditure was mainly financed through debt, resulting in higher budget deficits and overall public debt levels (see Chapter 1). Non-tax revenues increased only modestly and did not compensate for the fall in tax revenues.

Figure 2.9. Tax revenues, total revenues and government expenditure in the OECD

Taxes as a share of total revenue and total expenditure (left panel) and taxes, total revenue and expenditure as a share of GDP (right panel) – OECD unweighted average, 2000 – 2015

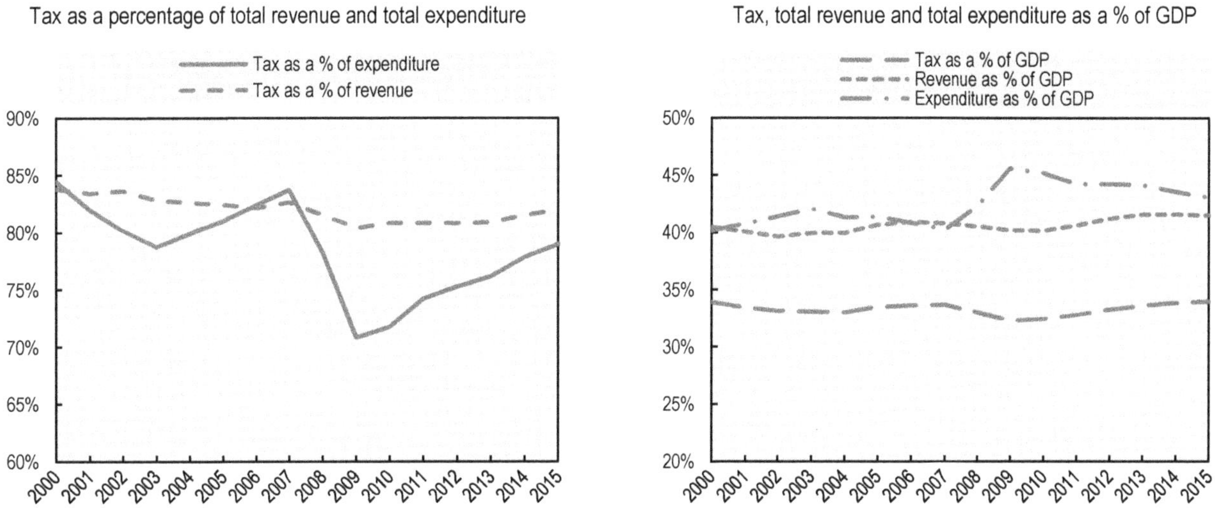

Source: "Special Feature" in (OECD, 2017[4]), *Revenue Statistics: 1965-2016.*

Recent years have seen a narrowing of the gap between levels of government expenditure and revenues. Total revenues as a share of GDP have increased since the crisis, reflecting an increase in both tax and non-tax revenues (Figure 2.9, right panel). But more significantly, there has been a strong decrease in public expenditure as a share of GDP. As a consequence of the strong decline in public spending and the increase in revenues as a share of GDP, the gap between government spending and revenues, and therefore budget deficits, have narrowed.

Between 2015 and 2016, most countries saw their tax revenues increase more (or decrease less) than public spending. Figure 2.10 looks at percentage point changes in tax revenues and government spending as a share of GDP between 2015 and 2016. In the countries that experienced tax increases, these were generally accompanied by either spending cuts or lower increases in public spending. Greece, in particular, in an effort to address its high debt-to-GDP ratio and meet the requirements under its bailout agreement, combined the strongest increase in tax revenues with the largest decrease in public spending as a share of GDP. In the countries that experienced tax revenue decreases, these were generally accompanied by even greater decreases in public spending, also indicating improvements in public budgets. There were a few exceptions, however, with public spending increasing more than tax revenues in Iceland, Norway, Canada and the United States, for instance.

Figure 2.10. Percentage point changes in tax revenues and government spending as a share of GDP between 2015 and 2016

P.p. changes in government spending (x axis) and in tax revenues (y axis) between 2015 and 2016 and gross government debt as a share of GDP in 2015 (size of the bubbles)

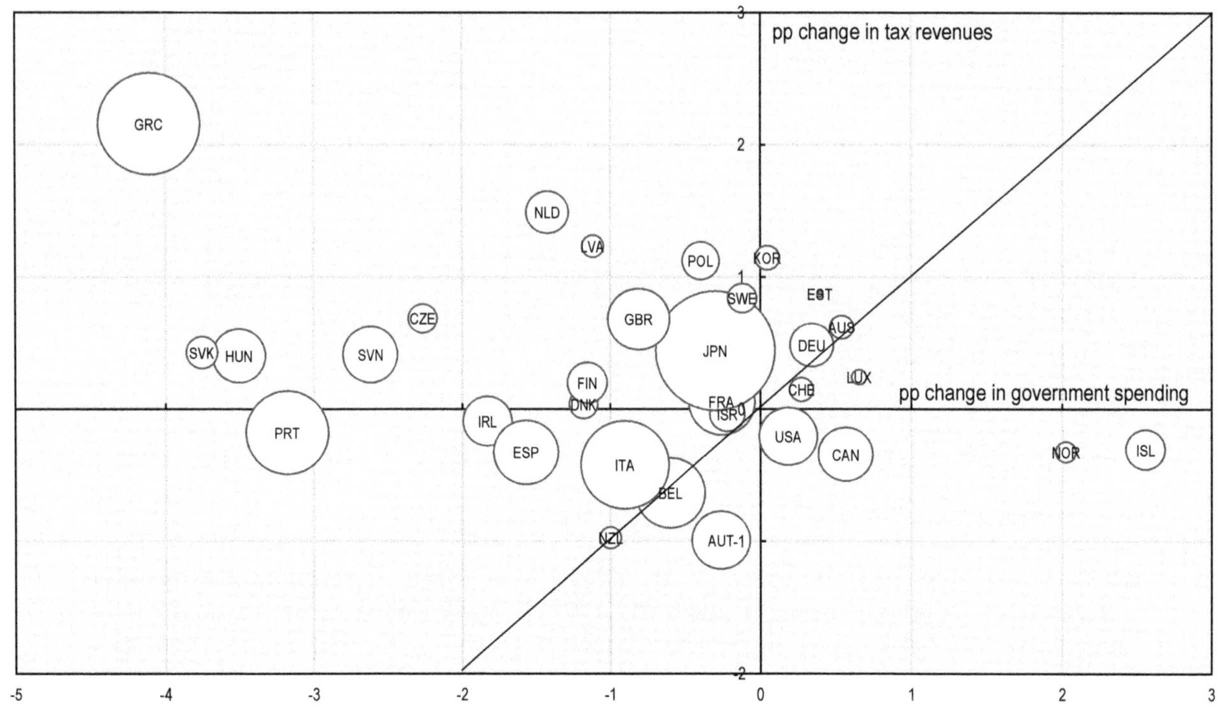

Note: No data for Argentina, Chile, Indonesia, Mexico, South Africa and Turkey. P.p. changes between 2014 and 2015 for Australia and Japan.
Source: OECD Economic Outlook 102 database and OECD Revenue Statistics database.

Changes in tax mixes

The composition of tax revenues varies across countries

The tax structures – or composition of total tax revenues – of countries vary quite significantly. As shown in Figure 2.11, income taxes – including both personal income tax (PIT) and corporate income tax (CIT) – are the largest source of tax revenues in 18 countries. In Denmark, Australia, New Zealand, South Africa and the United States, income taxes account for half or more of total tax revenues, which is partly explained by the fact that Australia, Denmark, New Zealand and South Africa do not collect (or collect very little) social security contributions (SSCs) and partly explained by the comparatively small share of consumption taxes in the United States. In a number of countries, including Central European countries and large Western European countries, SSCs are the primary source of tax revenues. There is a third group of countries which collect most of their tax revenues from consumption taxes.

Figure 2.11. Tax structures by country in 2015

Tax revenues expressed as a share of total taxation

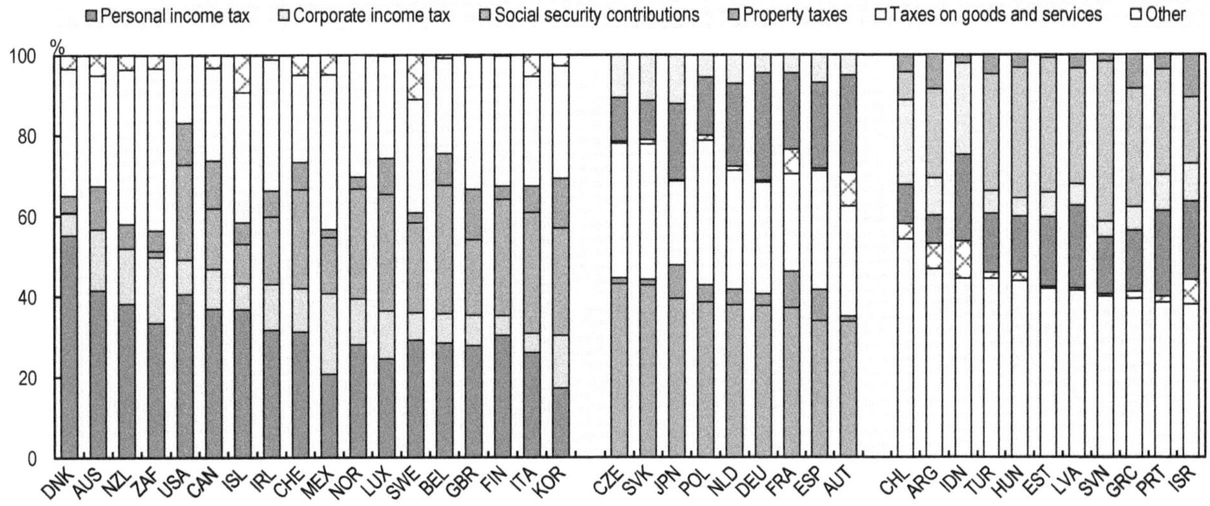

Note: Countries are grouped and ranked by those where income tax revenues (personal and corporate) form the higher share of total tax revenues, followed by those where SSCs, and taxes on goods and services, form the highest share.
Source: OECD and Global Revenue Statistics databases.

As with tax-to-GDP ratios, there tends to be a link between countries' tax mixes and GDP per capita levels. As shown in Figure 2.12 (left panel), the share of PIT in total tax revenues is positively correlated with countries' levels of GDP per capita, with more developed countries exhibiting higher shares of tax revenues from PIT. There are outliers, however, including South Africa which collects a large share of its total tax revenues through PIT but has a comparatively low level of GDP per capita. In contrast, the share of consumption tax revenues in the total tax mix tends to decrease when GDP per capita levels increase (Figure 2.12, right panel). CIT revenues (not shown in Figure 2.12) also tend to account for a larger share of total tax revenues in emerging economies than in more advanced countries.

Figure 2.12. Variation in the composition of tax revenues and levels of development

Personal income taxes as a share of total taxation and GDP per capita in 2016 (left panel) and consumption taxes as a share of total taxation and GDP per capita in 2016 (right panel)

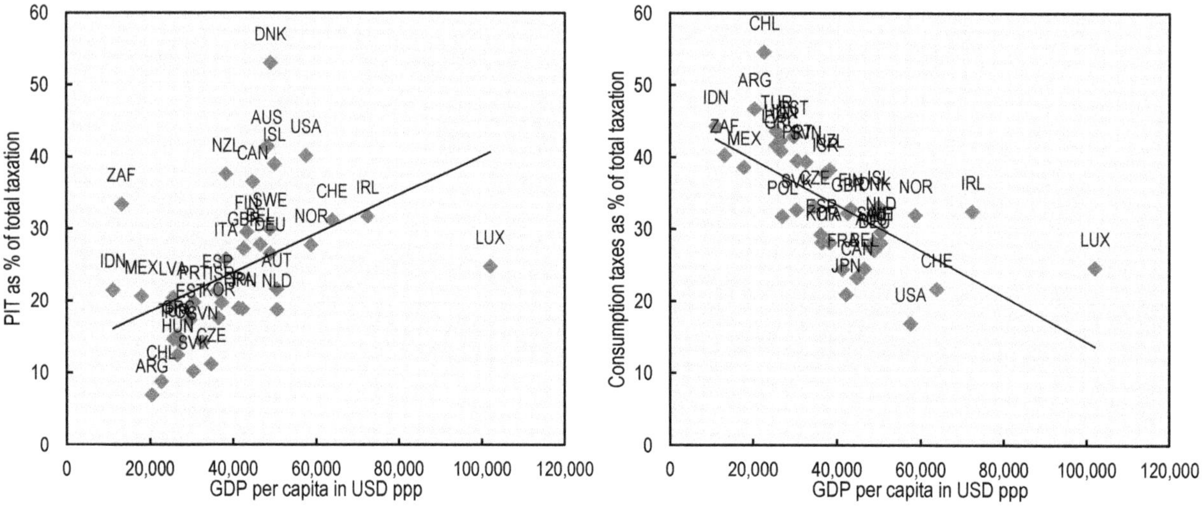

Note: For PIT revenues as a share of total taxation: 2015 data for Australia, Greece, Indonesia, Japan, Mexico and South Africa. For consumption tax revenues: 2015 data for Australia, Indonesia, Japan, Mexico and South Africa.

Source: OECD and Global Revenue Statistics databases and Aggregate National Accounts.

In recent years, personal income taxes have accounted for an increasing share of tax revenues

On average, the OECD's tax mix is dominated by SSCs, PIT and VAT. Overall in the OECD, SSCs and payroll taxes accounted for 27.0% of total tax revenues in 2015. PIT was the second largest source of tax revenues, accounting on average for 24.4% of total tax revenues. VAT also plays a major role, making up one fifth of the OECD's average tax mix in 2015, while other consumption taxes accounted for around 12.4% of the tax mix. On the other hand, taxes on corporate income and property are much less significant sources of tax revenues on average, respectively accounting for 8.9% and 5.8% of the OECD average tax mix in 2015 (Figure 2.13).

Figure 2.13. OECD average tax mix in 2000, 2007 and 2015

Tax revenues expressed as a share of total taxation

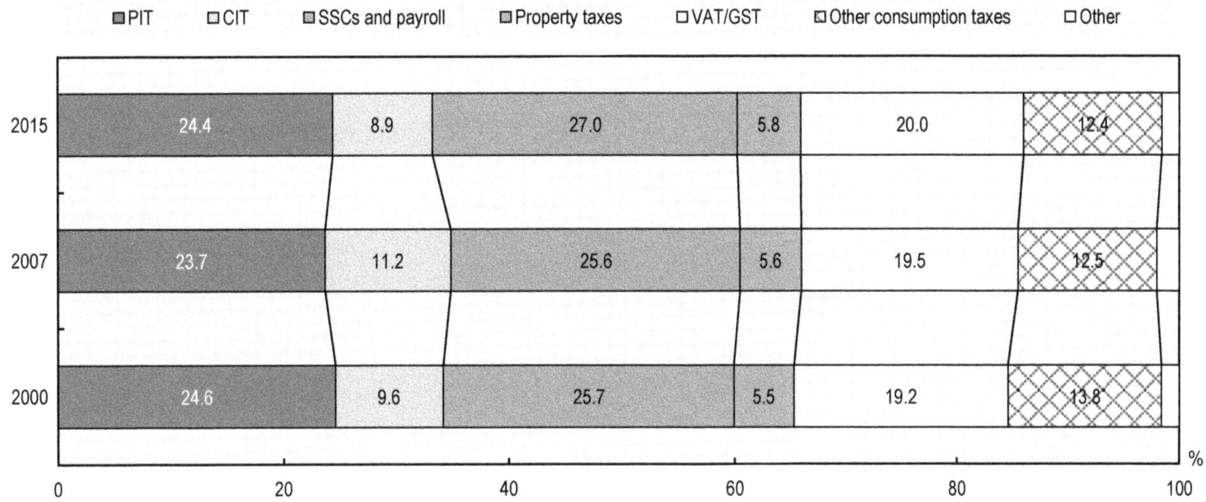

Source: OECD Revenue Statistics database.

Immediately after the crisis, there was a strong increase in revenues from VAT and SSCs. On average, the shares of SSCs and taxes on goods and services in total tax revenues rose to highs of 26.6% in 2009 and 33.0% in 2010 respectively. This partly reflected the effects of the tax reforms that were introduced in the wake of the crisis, in particular increases in SSCs and in standard VAT rates (OECD, 2016[3]). These trends also highlight the rapid revenue-raising effects of increases in SSCs and consumption taxes compared to other taxes. Since then, the shares of total tax revenues from SSCs and consumption taxes have steadily declined (Figure 2.14), but they remain larger sources of tax revenues on average than in 2007 (Figure 2.13).

Figure 2.14. Percentage point changes in tax revenues compared to their 2007 levels

OECD average, p.p. changes in tax revenues as a % of total tax revenues

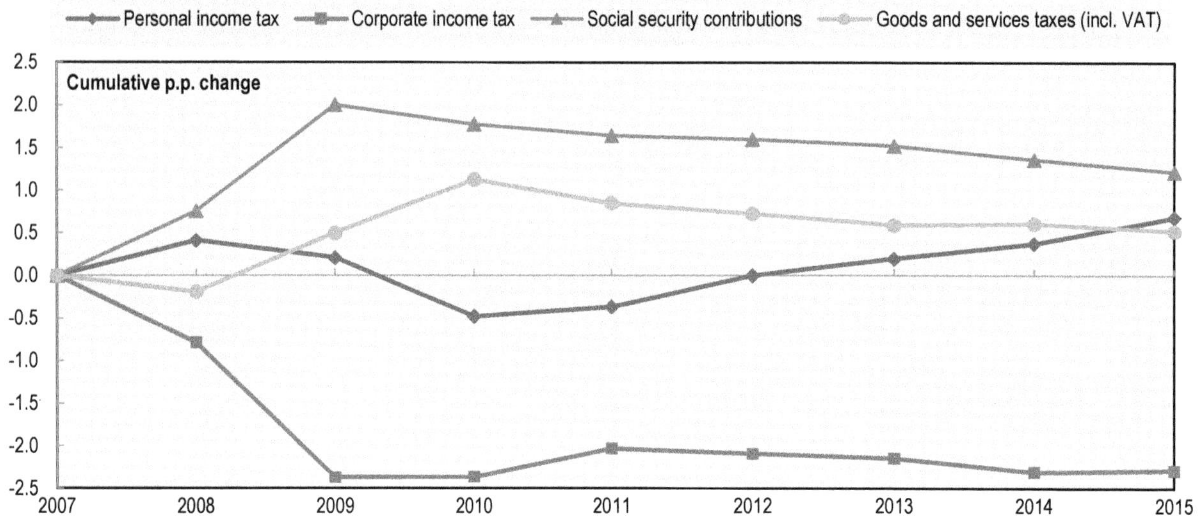

Source: OECD Revenue Statistics database.

More recently, PIT has been playing an increasingly significant role in the tax mix. In contrast with trends in SSC and VAT revenues, the share of PIT revenues in the OECD's average tax mix initially fell after the crisis, from 23.7% in 2007 to a low of 23.2% in 2010, but has been increasing steadily since then (Figure 2.14), partly reflecting the effects of PIT rate increases and PIT base broadening measures (OECD, 2016[3]). Between 2014 and 2015, the average share of PIT in total tax revenues increased from 24.1% to 24.4%. In 2015, PIT revenues accounted for a higher share of total tax revenues than in 2007 on average, but were still slightly below their 2000 level (Figure 2.13). As discussed in Chapter 3, however, the focus of PIT reforms has changed in the last couple of years, with many countries lowering taxes, in particular on low and middle income earners.

On the other hand, the importance of CIT in the OECD average tax mix has declined. On average across OECD countries, the share of tax revenues from CIT peaked at 11.2% in 2007, a year characterised by exceptional CIT revenues. In the following years, corporate tax revenues fell sharply, reaching a low of 8.8% in 2010. Since then, CIT revenues as a share of the OECD average tax mix have remained relatively stable (Figure 2.14). Accounting for 8.9% of tax revenues on average across OECD countries in 2015, CIT revenues are a smaller source of tax revenues than they used to be in 2000, when their share of the OECD's tax mix was equal to 9.6% (Figure 2.13).

Notes

[1] The report includes all OECD countries as at 1 January 2018.

[2] The countries covered in this report that we do not have 2016 tax revenue data for are: Australia, Indonesia, Japan and South Africa.

References

OECD (2017), *Revenue Statistics: 1965-2016*, OECD Publishing, Paris, http://dx.doi.org/10.1787/9789264283183-en. [1]

OECD (2017), *Revenue Statistics: 1965-2016*, OECD Publishing, Paris, http://dx.doi.org/10.1787/9789264283183-en. [4]

OECD (2017), *Tax Policy Reforms 2017: OECD and Selected Partner Economies*, OECD Publishing, Paris, http://dx.doi.org/10.1787/9789264279919-en. [2]

OECD (2016), *Tax Policy Reforms in the OECD 2016*, OECD Publishing, Paris, http://dx.doi.org/10.1787/9789264260399-en. [3]

OECD (2016), *Tax Policy Reforms in the OECD 2016*, OECD Publishing, Paris, http://dx.doi.org/10.1787/9789264260399-en. [5]

Chapter 3. The latest tax policy reforms

This chapter provides an overview of the latest tax reforms in OECD countries, Argentina, Indonesia and South Africa. It identifies the most significant tax reforms that were introduced as well as common tax policy trends across groups of countries. It looks at trends in each category of tax separately, including personal income taxes and social security contributions, corporate income taxes, VAT/GST and excise duties, environmentally related taxes and property taxes.

This chapter provides an overview of the latest tax reforms in all OECD countries[1] as well as in Argentina, Indonesia and South Africa. It identifies the most significant tax reforms that have recently been introduced as well as common tax policy trends across groups of countries. It examines trends in each category of tax including personal income taxes and social security contributions (Section 3.1), corporate income taxes and other corporate taxes (Section 3.2), VAT/GST and non-energy excise duties (Section 3.3.), environmentally-related taxes (Section 3.4) and property taxes (Section 3.5).

The discussion in this chapter is primarily based on countries' responses to the 2018 Annual Tax Policy Reform Questionnaire which requested information on countries' latest tax reforms. The questionnaire asked responding countries to describe the reforms as well as to provide details on their expected revenue effects and other relevant information, including the rationale for the tax measures (see Box 3.1).

Box 3.1. The OECD Annual Tax Policy Reform Questionnaire

At the Working Party No.2 on Tax Policy Analysis and Tax Statistics (WP2) meeting in November 2009, delegates from OECD countries agreed to start collecting more systematic information on the main tax measures adopted in each country. The motivation for this proposal was to provide consistent and comparative information on tax reforms to inform policy discussions in OECD and non-OECD countries.

At the November 2010 WP2 meeting, the following criteria were agreed for deciding whether a tax policy measure was sufficiently substantial to be reported in the questionnaire:

- A significant change in a tax rate;
- A change in the tax base that is expected to change revenue from that base by more than 5% or 0.1% of GDP; and
- A politically important systemic reform.

Any central or sub-central tax policy measure that was *implemented, legislated or announced* in the previous *calendar* year which meets at least one of the criteria listed above must be reported in the questionnaire.

For each reform, the questionnaire requests information on the type of tax; the dates of entry into force, legislation or announcement; the direction of the rate and/or base change; and a detailed description of the reform. The questionnaire also asks for the rationale behind the reform and estimates of the revenue effects of the tax measures.

This questionnaire forms the basis of this report, which is the third edition of the annual *Tax Policy Reforms: OECD and Selected Partner Economies* publication.

Personal income taxes and social security contributions

In the area of personal income tax (PIT), the report confirms the trend towards tax cuts on labour income, after years of gradual PIT increases following the crisis. It is therefore unsurprising that most of the reforms are expected to reduce tax revenues in the short term. A rationale cited by many countries for introducing these reforms has been to enhance fairness. One pattern of reform has been to increase earned income tax credits (EITCs), which have the potential to improve labour market participation and enhance PIT progressivity. In parallel, the trend towards higher tax rates on personal capital income has continued, although some countries have expanded tax reliefs for some forms of financial income. From a country perspective, the most significant reforms were introduced in the United States with changes in PIT rates and deductions, Latvia with the introduction of a progressive PIT system, and France with a new flat tax on personal capital income. The Netherlands has also announced major PIT reforms as part of its coalition agreement.

Regarding social security contributions (SSCs), rate changes have been broadly evenly split between cuts and increases as have base changes between broadening and narrowing measures. Compared to recent years, however, one development has been a greater focus on SSC rate increases and base narrowing, which suggests that greater contributions will be placed upon a smaller number of contributors in some countries. More generally, despite SSCs weighing heavily on labour income in many countries, efforts to shift tax mixes away from SSCs have been limited.

Labour taxes are the most important source of tax revenues in OECD countries on average

When combined, PIT and SSCs are the most important source of tax revenues in most countries. Together, they account for half of tax revenues in OECD countries on average and for a third in Argentina and South Africa. As shown in Figure 3.1, in 2016, they accounted for over 60% of tax revenue in Germany, the United States, Austria and Sweden and about 40% in Israel, New Zealand and Mexico. In Chile, which is somewhat of an exception, their share of total tax revenues was 14%. In the Slovak Republic, the Czech Republic and Slovenia, SSCs alone accounted for over 40% of total taxation. In Denmark, Australia and the United States, PIT alone accounted for over 40% of total tax revenues.

Figure 3.1. PIT, SSCs and payroll taxes as a share of total tax revenues by country, 2016

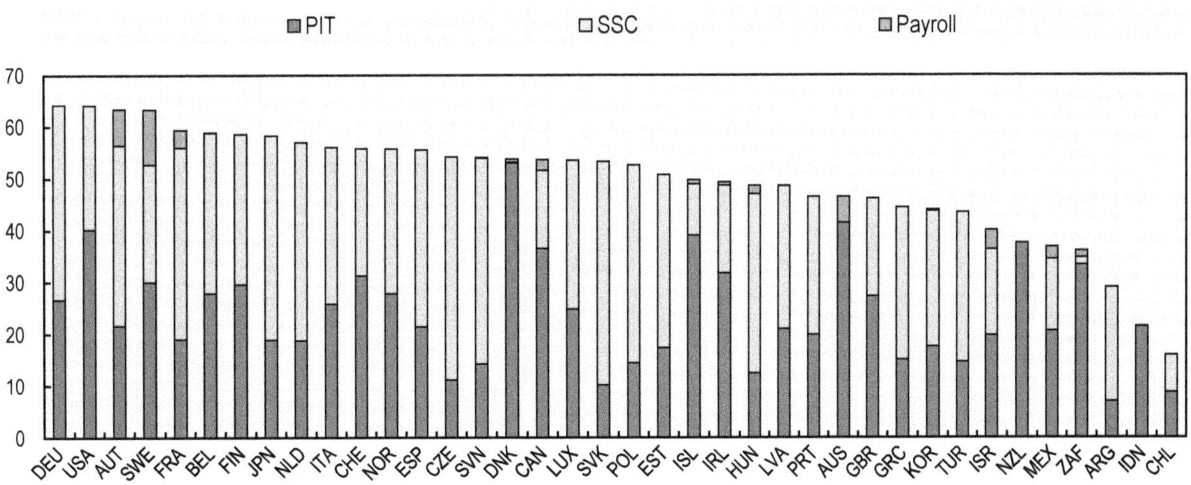

Note: 2015 data for Australia, Greece, Indonesia, Japan, Mexico and South Africa. In Indonesia, data on SSCs are currently unavailable.
Source: OECD and Global Revenue Statistics databases.

The composition of labour tax revenue has evolved over time among OECD countries, with SSCs gradually overtaking PIT as the most important source of tax revenue. Over the past 50 years, PIT has gradually declined as a share of total revenue while SSCs have gradually increased (Figure 3.2). In 1965, SSCs comprised 17.6% of tax revenues on average while PIT comprised 26.2%. By 1995, they were about equal at approximately 25%. In 2015, SSCs represented 25.8% of total tax revenues on average, surpassing the PIT share of 24.4%. The sum of PIT and SSCs has remained relatively constant over time, typically at around half of tax revenue, but the mix has changed.

Figure 3.2. PIT, SSCs and payroll tax revenues as a share of total taxation, OECD average, 1965-2015

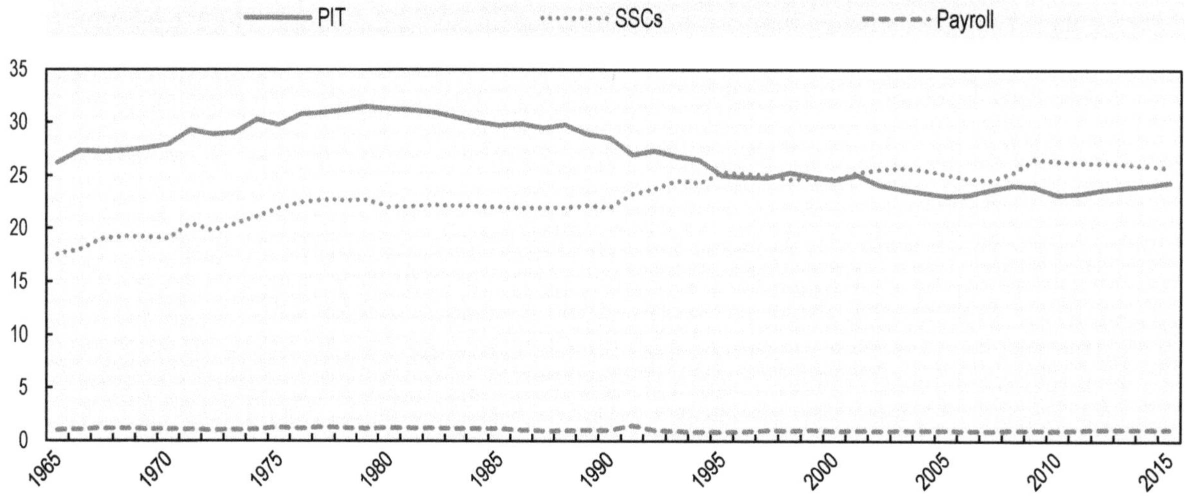

Source: OECD Revenue Statistics database.

Taxes on labour income declined on average between 2013 and 2017, after a series of post-crisis increases

The average tax burden on labour income declined between 2000 and 2009 and increased sharply after the economic crisis before declining again in recent years (Figure 3.3). Between 2009 and 2013, the OECD average tax wedge – the total tax payments on labour income as a percentage of labour costs – for single workers earning the average wage increased by one percentage point, from 35.2% to 36.2%. This was mainly a reflection of countries' fiscal consolidation efforts. In recent years, the tax wedge has declined, albeit modestly, reaching 35.9% in 2017 (OECD, 2018[1]).

Figure 3.3. Evolution of the average tax wedge on labour income in the OECD between 2000 and 2017

Average tax wedge for a single person without children earning 100% of the average wage, expressed as a share of labour costs

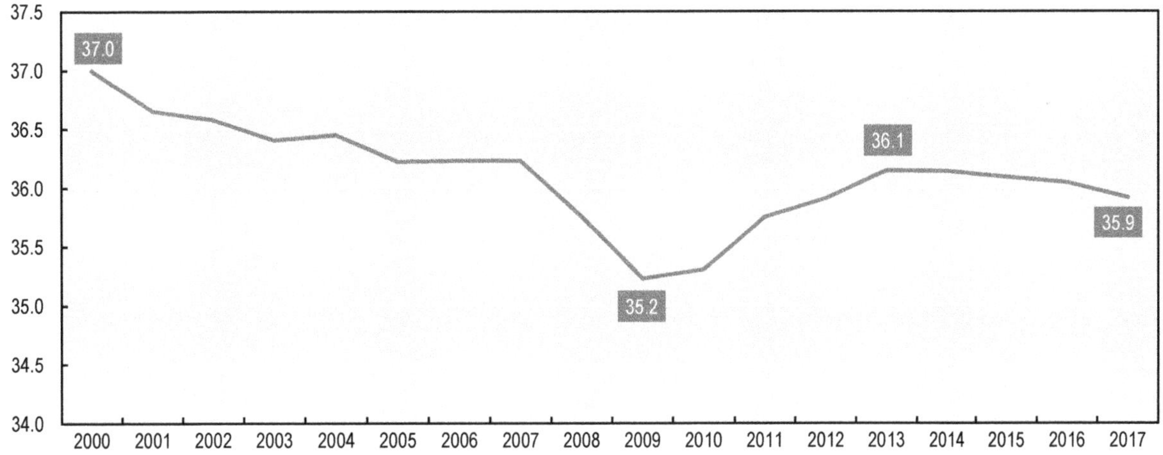

Source: OECD Taxing Wages Database.

Figure 3.4 shows that the same general trends hold across family types. In the early 2000s, the tax burden declined, particularly for families with children. After the crisis period, tax wedges rose across all family types, particularly for one-earner married couples with children. Nevertheless, tax wedges remain lower across family types than in the early 2000s.

Figure 3.4. Changes in labour income tax wedges in OECD countries before and after the financial crisis by family type

Percentage point changes

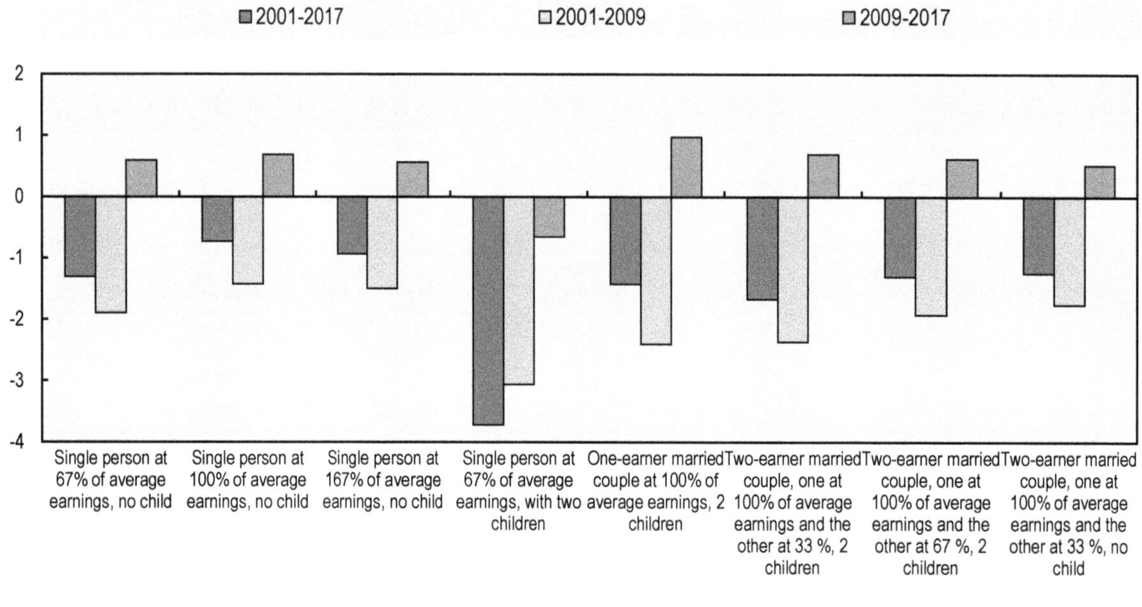

Source: OECD Taxing Wages Database.

Despite an overall declining trend, the average tax wedge increased in some countries between 2016 and 2017 as shown in Figure 3.5. For example, the tax wedge increased in Turkey, the Czech Republic, Mexico, Greece, Latvia, Slovenia and Ireland. In Hungary, Luxembourg, Finland, Iceland, Canada and France, there were significant reductions in the tax wedge.

Figure 3.5. Change in tax wedge and its components across OECD countries between 2016 and 2017

Percentage point changes

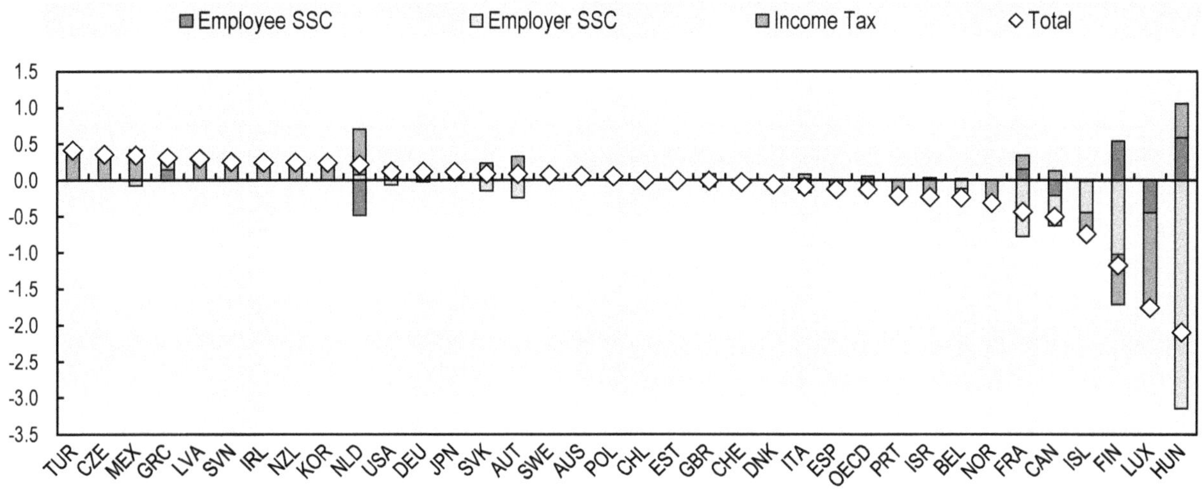

Note: Single individuals without children at the average wage level. Employer SSC includes payroll taxes where applicable.
Source: OECD Taxing Wages Database.

A majority of countries are cutting PIT rates

A number of PIT policy options are available to governments to achieve various objectives including raising tax revenues, increasing economic growth or enhancing the redistributive impact of the tax system. These options involve the upward or downward adjustment of PIT rates and the broadening or narrowing of PIT bases. At the heart of these policy choices, there is often a trade-off between equity and efficiency. On the one hand, the PIT represents the main source of progressivity in the tax systems of most countries and tax rate increases on the upper income brackets have the potential to enhance fairness by shifting the burden from lower to higher incomes. On the other hand, rate increases can reduce economic incentives to work, save and invest. This section will look at the PIT reforms that were recently introduced in OECD countries, beginning with PIT rate reforms followed by PIT base changes.

Top PIT rate reforms are evenly split between cuts and increases

Of the countries undertaking top PIT rate reforms, four reforms involved tax rate cuts and four involved tax rate increases. The numbers and direction of these reforms closely follow reform trends in recent years. In 2017 for example, four countries reported top PIT rate cuts and five reported top PIT rate increases (Table 3.1).

Table 3.1. PIT rate reforms introduced in 2017 and 2018

	Rate ⇧		Rate ⇩	
Of which	**2017**	**2018 or later**	**2017**	**2018 or later**
Top PIT rate	ISR KOR LUX NOR	CAN[1] KOR LVA ZAF	FIN IRL[2] NOR PRT	FIN (NLD) NOR[4] PRT[5] USA
Non-top PIT rate(s)	AUS LUX NLD	DNK KOR SWE[3]	ARG BEL FIN FRA HUN IRL ISL ISR LUX PRT SVN	CAN[1] FIN GRC IRL LVA (NLD) NOR[4] PRT[5] USA

Note: Countries in brackets have only announced reforms.
[1] In Canada, a new top PIT rate was introduced in British Columbia while in Saskatchewan and Quebec there were PIT rate reductions.
[2] Ireland reduced the universal social charge.
[3] In Sweden, there was a PIT increase for non-residents.
[4] In Norway, the tax rates on ordinary income for individuals were reduced while the rates for personal income were increased.
[5] In Portugal, the PIT surtax was eliminated.
Source: OECD Annual Tax Policy Reform Questionnaire.

Among the countries cutting top PIT rates, the Tax Cuts and Jobs Act in the United States represents the most significant reform. In the United States, the federal top tax rate[2], which applies to single filers with income over USD 500 000 and married joint filers with income over USD 600 000, was reduced from 39.6% to 37%. The Netherlands announced a top rate cut of similar magnitude from 52% to 49.5% for 2019. In Norway, Finland and Portugal, the top PIT rate cuts were significantly smaller and part of more general PIT rate decreases affecting all tax brackets (see below). Overall, countries expect these cuts to decrease tax revenues in the short-term.

Of the countries increasing their top PIT rate, Latvia introduced a major reform by replacing its flat rate income tax system with a new progressive income tax system from 1 January 2018. Previously, the PIT rate was 23% for all earners. As part of the new reform, PIT rates are 20% on income up to EUR 20 004, 23% on income from EUR 20 004 to EUR 55 000 and 31.4% on income over EUR 55 000. The reform is expected to reduce tax revenues in part due to a relatively large proportion of taxpayers in the lower tax bracket that may now be taxed at the newly enacted lower rate. A stated objective of the reform, which is part of a more comprehensive tax reform (see Box 3.2), is to alleviate income inequality.

Other countries have increased their top PIT rates including South Africa, which increased its rate significantly from 41% to 45% and Korea which raised the top PIT rate from 40% to 42% (for taxable income above KRW 500 million). While there have been varied rate reforms across provinces in Canada, British Columbia has introduced a new PIT rate (and threshold) of 16.8% for taxable income exceeding CAD 150 000.

Tax rate cuts targeted at low and middle-income earners have continued

Unlike the top PIT rate reforms, where there was an equal split between rate cuts and increases, the vast majority of countries that have undertaken non-top PIT rate reforms have cut them: eight countries reported cuts and two countries reported increases. Overall, the rate changes were relatively small, however. As was the case for top PIT rates, these broadly follow recent tax reform trends. In 2017 for example, eleven countries reported cuts and two reported increases (Table 3.1).

In some countries, PIT rate cuts across the middle and lower tax bands were part of significant changes in PIT rate schedules. In the United States, the tax reform maintained the seven-bracket PIT structure but modified PIT rates and the income levels to which they apply. Generally, the reform lowered PIT rates, with new rates of 10%, 12%, 22%, 24%, 32%, 35% and 37%. In Portugal, the number of tax brackets will increase from five to seven. There is a new band between EUR 7 091 and EUR 10 700 with a PIT rate of 23% and between EUR 20 261 and EUR 25 000 with a rate of 35% (the minimum and maximum rates are being maintained up to a top rate of 48%). The reform is expected to modestly reduce tax revenues. In addition, the surtax, which is an additional tax on earned income subject to PIT introduced during the economic crisis, was abolished in 2017. The Netherlands also announced that the number of brackets will be halved from four to two and the rate of the first bracket will be 36.95%. This reform is expected to reduce income taxes, particularly for middle and high income earners.

In Norway, various PIT rate changes have been introduced, overall leading to a slight decrease in marginal tax rates. The Norwegian tax system has two income bases; ordinary income which has a net base and personal income which has a gross base. The tax rate on ordinary income will be reduced from 24% to 23%. At the same time, rates on personal income for employees have increased marginally at each bracket, which will partly fund the decrease in the rate on ordinary income. Overall, marginal PIT rates are expected to decrease slightly.

In Greece, the income tax schedule is being largely maintained but a cut in the rate on the first band from 22% to 20% is planned from January 2020. The reform, which is expected to decrease tax revenues, aims in part to alleviate the tax burden on small unincorporated businesses. In addition, the solidarity surcharge will be imposed on income of more than EUR 30 000 from 2020 onwards, an increase from its previous level of EUR 12 000. However, these measures are conditional upon a budget evaluation by the IMF, the European Commission, the European Central Bank, the European Stability Mechanism and the Greek authorities.

Other non-top PIT rate cuts were introduced in Canada, Ireland and Finland. While there have been varied rate reforms across provinces in Canada, in Saskatchewan there has been an overall reduction of 1% for each PIT rate over the period 2017 to 2020. In Quebec, there is a reduction in the PIT rate from 16% to 15% in the first taxable income bracket. In Ireland, the Universal Social Charge (USC), which is a tax on all income (if income is above EUR 13 000), has been marginally reduced at various bands. The new USC rates are 0.5% up to EUR 12 012, 2% between EUR 12 012 and EUR 19 372, 4.75% between EUR 19 372 and EUR 70 044 and 8% for incomes over EUR 70 044. Incomes of EUR 13 000 or less will continue to be exempt from the USC in 2018. In Finland, there is set to be a reduction of all marginal tax rates on earned income by 0.25%. This is in part to compensate wage earners for an increase in SSCs.

Only three countries raised non-top PIT rates. Korea introduced a new PIT bracket for individuals with taxable income between KRW 300 million and KRW 500 million. In Sweden, with a view to raising revenues, the special PIT rate for non-residents has been raised from 20% to 25%. In Denmark, a gradual increase in the bottom PIT rate was introduced to finance the elimination of the Public Service Obligation (PSO) tax, which has been used to support renewable energy.

Box 3.2. Latvia's comprehensive tax reform

The Latvian Parliament adopted a tax reform in the summer of 2017, which came into force in 2018. The three main goals of the reform as reported by the Latvian government include supporting economic growth, addressing income inequality and ensuring that tax revenues are sufficiently high to finance government priorities. The most significant changes introduced by the reform are in the area of direct taxation, with accompanying consumption and capital income tax measures.

Regarding personal income tax, the most significant change is the repeal of the flat tax and the introduction of a progressive income tax system for labour income. Additional measures include increasing the differential non-taxable minimum, the allowance for dependents and the non-taxable minimum income for pensioners. SSCs will be raised by 1 percentage point to finance healthcare services. Overall, labour tax measures will strengthen tax wedge progressivity, in particular through a large decrease in the tax burden on low-income earners with no dependents.

With regard to corporate taxes, the biggest change involves deferring CIT to the moment profits are distributed as CIT will only be payable on distributed profits and not on profits that are re-invested. To partially compensate for this significant base change, the CIT rate will be raised from 15% to 20%. The CIT taxable period will also be changed to one month. There will be a number of special provisions to ensure the transition to the new corporate tax system.

On the other hand, revenue-raising measures include increasing the PIT rate on capital income to 20%, increasing excise duty rates as well as gambling tax rates, and restricting the micro-enterprise tax regime.

With respect to revenue effects, the reform is expected to cause a considerable initial drop in CIT revenues, followed by a moderate rebound in subsequent years, an increase in VAT and excise duty revenues, a medium-term decrease in PIT revenues, and an increase in SSC revenues.

Countries continue to narrow PIT tax bases particularly through expanded EITCs

A majority of PIT base reforms in 2018 have been targeted to support employment and low-income earners. Overall, these measures narrow the tax base and are expected to reduce tax revenues. However, many countries simultaneously introduced mixed reforms that broadened and narrowed the tax base at the same time. Of the countries undertaking tax base reforms, 27 were base narrowing and nine were base broadening. Compared to tax base reforms in 2017, the number and direction of these adjustments is very similar when there were 32 reforms that narrowed bases and 11 that broadened them.

One pattern of reform adopted by a number of countries was to increase EITCs, which have the potential to improve labour market participation, reduce poverty and enhance progressivity. A risk with such measures, however, is that unless they are well designed, they can reduce work incentives for those already in employment, in addition to coming at a high fiscal cost. A further important trend has been the increase in basic allowances. There were also several age-related measures to provide income support to low income older people.

Table 3.2. PIT base reforms introduced in 2017 and 2018

	Base ⇧		Base ⇩	
Of which	2017	2018 or later	2017	2018 or later
Personal allowances, credits, tax brackets	AUS LUX SWE	GRC JPN USA	ARG DEU EST BEL FIN GBR IRL LUX LVA NOR NLD SVN	CAN IRL JPN LVA NLD NOR PRT SVN TUR USA
Targeted low-income/EITCs	NLD	NLD	FIN IRL LUX POL	CAN FIN IRL ITA NLD
Children & other dependents			AUS (CZE) DEU HUN IRL LUX	IRL ISL LVA USA
Elderly & disabled		NLD	NLD	LVA NLD SWE
Miscellaneous expenses & deductions	AUS CAN (CZE) EST GBR LUX SWE	LVA NLD NOR USA	BEL EST FIN HUN ISL LUX PRT SVK SWE	MEX[1] NOR SVN SWE TUR

Note: Countries in brackets have only announced reforms.

[1] In Mexico, a range of measures were introduced to support the victims of earthquakes in the most affected areas.

Source: OECD Annual Tax Policy Reform Questionnaire.

General tax allowances and credits

The first and largest category of reforms to PIT bases relates to personal tax allowances and credits. In this category, there were a total of ten base narrowing and three base broadening reforms, similar to 2017.

In the United States, the standard deduction was almost doubled for individuals (to USD 12 000), single parents (USD 18 000) and married couples (USD 24 000). This measure is intended to boost growth. At the same time, however, the personal exemptions were eliminated. These measures were introduced with a sunset clause which is scheduled to take effect in 2025.

In Japan, the basic allowance that applies to all taxpayers will rise from JPY 380 000 to JPY 480 000 in January 2020. This measure will be partly funded by cutting the income-related allowance for salaried workers by JPY 100 000, uniformly for all salaried workers. The measure is also intended to reduce the effect of the tax system on choices between salaried jobs and different types of non-salaried jobs. In addition to this measure, the maximum amount for the income-related allowance for salaried workers will be lowered. This will lead to an increase in income tax for workers earning more than JPY 8.5 million (USD 75 400). However, the amount of income tax will not be increased if the taxpayer supports children and relatives who need nursing care.

Increases in basic allowances and other general deductions have been introduced in other countries. In Quebec, Canada, the basic personal amount is raised from CAD 11 635 to CAD 14 890. The basic personal allowance for wage income (and social security) has also increased in Norway. In Slovenia, a general tax relief was introduced for incomes between EUR 11 166 and EUR 13 317. In Turkey, the minimum living allowance will be increased for certain minimum wage earners who move into the second tax bracket and their net income falls below the minimum wage. In Ireland, the point of entry to the higher rate of income tax was increased by EUR 750 for all earners. For single individuals, the income tax standard rate band was increased from EUR 33 800 to EUR 34 550 and for married one earner couples it was increased from EUR 42 800 to EUR 43 550. The Netherlands has also announced that the general tax credit will be increased gradually.

On the other hand, Greece is broadening its PIT base by significantly reducing child tax credits from 2020, which is anticipated to raise tax revenues. For example, for taxpayers with one child, tax credits are reduced from EUR 1 950 to EUR 1 300 and for those with two children they are reduced from EUR 2 000 to EUR 1 350. This broadening may be offset to an extent by the aforementioned PIT rate cut in Greece on the first tax band from 22% to 20%.

Earned income tax credits

The second largest category of PIT base reforms is related to earned income tax credits (EITCs), which aim at supporting workers on low incomes. Designed correctly, such credits have the potential to improve labour market participation and reduce poverty. In 2018, most countries reforming EITCs have expanded their scope.

Changes to EITCs were introduced in Canada, Finland, Ireland, Italy and the Netherlands. In Canada, the working income tax benefit will be replaced by the Canada Worker Benefit (CWB) to support the benefits provided to low-income workers. The maximum benefits have been increased for both families and singles without dependents to support low-income workers. In Finland, there has been an increase in the EITC from EUR 1 420 to EUR 1 540 to be introduced in 2020. In Ireland, the EITC for self-employed was increased from EUR 950 to EUR 1 150 although this remains below the EUR 1 650 tax credit for PAYE workers. In Italy, with effect from 2018, the EITC for employees was expanded to encourage consumption and increase fairness in the tax system, with an increase in the entitlement threshold to the full amount of the credit from EUR 24 000 to EUR 24 600. The Netherlands undertook reforms that both narrowed and broadened the tax base at the same time. The maximum of the (income dependent) EITC will be increased gradually by approximately EUR 545 in total. The same credit will decrease by 6.0% for every euro earned above EUR 33 112, which is expected to partly offset the decrease in tax revenues.

Children and other dependents

Four countries have expanded tax provisions targeted at those supporting children (and other dependents) in 2018. In the United States, the child tax credit is doubled to USD 2 000 per child (under 17) and a new tax credit of USD 500 is introduced for dependents (aged 17 or over). Israel also increased the tax credit for parents of children up to five years old. In Latvia, there was an increase in the allowance for dependents up to EUR 200 in 2018 (EUR 230 in 2019 and EUR 250 in 2020) and in Ireland the home carer tax credit increased from EUR 1 100 to EUR 1 200 to assist single-income families with caring responsibilities at home.

Elderly and the disabled

The fourth tax base reform category includes measures targeted at the elderly and the disabled. The most common policy rationale for age-related concessions is to provide income support to low income older people (OECD, 2011[2]). In 2018, three such reforms narrowed the tax base compared to just one in 2017. In Sweden, there were substantial tax base reforms to support the elderly and the disabled. For example, there was an increase in the basic allowance for individuals over the age of 65 in 2018 in addition to a further tax reduction for the elderly from 2019. There was also a tax reduction for disability. In the Netherlands, the general old age tax credit will be increased in 2018 and 2019 whereas the additional old age tax credit for single persons will decrease marginally. In Latvia, there is also an increase in the PIT non-taxable minimum for pensioners.

Incentives for highly skilled workers

Various reforms were also introduced to attract or retain the highly skilled. Many OECD countries already have such provisions in place (see Box 3.3). These kinds of reforms can help retain high-skilled workers and address skill shortages. In Turkey, with a view to supporting a more qualified workforce, a deduction was provided for employees in certain companies which provide services abroad. In Slovenia, a special tax scheme was introduced for income from employment of posting employees abroad. In addition, performance bonuses are exempt up to the average monthly wage in Slovenia. In Norway, there was a tax scheme for long-term investments in start-up companies and also a reduced taxation of employee options for small start-up companies. A further measure in Sweden included a reduced tax on employee share options in certain cases.

Base broadening measures among countries reducing PIT rates

Some of the countries reducing PIT rates or expanding tax benefits have also introduced base broadening reforms. In the United States, the revenue cost associated with the aforementioned increases in the standard deduction and child tax credits will partly be offset by temporarily modifying or eliminating certain tax preferences. These include capping the home mortgage interest deduction to interest expenses attributable to mortgage balances no greater than USD 750 000, eliminating deductions for home equity loan interest, and capping the deduction for state and local taxes at USD 10 000. In the Netherlands, as part of the coalition agreement, the plan is to gradually limit the rate of deductibility of most deductible items. In Norway, the tax base has been broadened through the abolition of the tax exemption for employees on shipping vessels in addition to limitations on the rules for commuter expenses. In Latvia, there was also a new limitation introduced on deductible expenses for education and medical services as well as donations.

Some countries introduced reforms to support self-employed workers and unincorporated businesses

There were a number of reforms targeted at self-employed workers and unincorporated businesses. In Italy, entrepreneurs, self-employed individuals, general partnerships and limited partnerships, will have the option to be taxed under a new entrepreneurial income tax (IRI). Under the IRI, business income that is reinvested will be excluded from individual taxable income and subject to separate taxation at the rate of 24%, which is equal to the CIT rate. The rationale for the reform was in part to have neutral tax treatment for different legal forms of business. The measure will become effective next year (on 2018 income). In the United States, taxpayers may deduct 20% of qualified pass-through income with certain limitations. For example, the limitations do not apply if the taxable income is less than USD 157 000 (single) or USD 315 000 (married). In addition, pass-through losses are disallowed if they exceed USD 500 000 for joint filers and USD 250 000 for all others. In Germany, to encourage investment, there was an increase in the value limit for the immediate write-off of low cost assets to EUR 800.

Box 3.3. Country examples of tax provisions for the highly skilled

This box examines selected country examples of tax provisions for the highly skilled. For example, Belgium exempts any labour and capital foreign source income received by foreign specialists and researchers for up to 20 years. Spain exempts foreign source income received by foreign employees occupying a managerial position. Foreign individuals moving to France receive a 50% tax exemption over foreign source passive income for up to 8 years. In the Netherlands, highly-skilled foreign workers may receive 30% of their wage untaxed to compensate for the costs of living abroad. They can use this exemption for up to 8 years, but it has recently been announced that this period would be reduced to 5 years. Belgium, Switzerland, France, Israel, Luxembourg and Sweden give highly-skilled workers a total exemption over fringe benefits related to their relocation and stay in the country. The table highlights selected examples of countries that provide reduced PIT rates and exemptions.

Reduced PIT rates and exemption of labour income from PIT

	Target	Years	Tax relief	Conditions
Iceland*	Highly-skilled workers	3	Taxed only over 75% of their income	Not been residents in the country for at least 5 years ; expertise that is limited or non-existent in the country
Sweden	Highly-skilled workers	3	Taxed only over 75% of their income	Not been residents in the country for at least 5 years
Canada*	Researchers working in R&D; professors	5	100% for the first two years, 75% for the third year, 50% for the fourth, 25% for the fifth	Not previously resident in Canada prior to taking up the position as an employee and settling in Quebec
Italy*	Workers with a university degree	4	Abatement of 50% of taxable income	To have resided at least for 5 years in a foreign country; to transfer the tax residence to Italy with the intention to remain in the country for at least 2 years
Italy*	Researchers	4	Exemption of PIT over 90% of the income	Working abroad for at least 2 years and becoming tax residents in the country for at least 2 years
Korea	Foreign technicians working in R&D	2	Exemption of PIT 50%	
The Netherlands	Highly-skilled foreign workers	8	Free allowance of up to 30% of the employment income	Expertise that is scarce or not available in the Dutch labour market
Denmark*	Workers fulfilling specific conditions and highly-paid employees	5	26% reduced PIT rate	To have not been tax residents in the country for at least 10 years and who are engaged in research at a university or in a private enterprise
Spain*	Foreign employees	5	24% reduced PIT rate	With income of up to EUR 600 000
Portugal*	Non-regular resident employees working on high value-added scientific, artistic or technical activities	10	20% reduced flat PIT rate	Individuals who have not been residents in Portugal in the previous 5 years

* means that these countries target not-nationals highly-skilled workers, and also grant tax benefits to returning nationals who have been non-residents in the country for a fixed period of time.

Increases in tax rates on personal capital income have continued, but some countries have expanded tax reliefs for financial income

Overall, the trend towards higher tax rates on personal capital income has continued, but some countries have expanded tax reliefs for some forms of financial income. Consequently, the revenue effects of the reforms are somewhat unclear. Tax increases on personal capital income were generally introduced to raise revenue and enhance fairness. On the other hand, tax relief seeks to support savings and investment, with a few countries aiming to lower the tax burden on small savers. In general, however, there is still significant scope to improve the effectiveness of the taxation of personal capital income in many countries (see Box 3.4).

A number of countries have raised taxes on personal capital income, in particular through tax rate increases

A number of countries have raised their tax rates on personal capital income, often to simultaneously raise revenue and enhance fairness (Table 3.3). In Latvia, the PIT rate on capital income and capital gains is raised from 10% and 15% to a unified rate of 20%. In Iceland, with the objective of raising revenue and narrowing the gap between the taxation of labour and capital income, the capital income tax rate was raised from 20% to 22%. In Argentina, exemptions for financial income were removed: interest and capital gains from different types of investments will be subject to a tax rate of 5% (for investments denominated in local currency without adjustment clauses) or 15% (for investments denominated in foreign currency, or in local currency with adjustment clauses) as from 1 January 2018. Argentina also introduced an additional withholding tax on distributed dividends (see Section 3.2). With a view to increasing the taxation of high capital income earners, Korea raised the tax rate on large shareholders whose capital gains exceed KRW 300 million from 20% to 25%. In the Netherlands, the government has announced an increase in the tax rate for income from substantial shareholdings (referred to as Box 2 income) from 25% to 28.5% as from 2021 onwards, in connection with the decrease in the CIT rate.

Table 3.3. Changes to tax rates on personal capital income introduced in 2017 and 2018

	Rate ⇧		Rate ⇩	
Of which	2017	2018 or later	2017	2018 or later
Dividend or interest income/equity or bond investment	BEL LUX NOR SVK	ARG ISL LVA (NLD)[2]	IRL	FRA
Capital gains		ARG ISL LVA (NLD)[2] KOR	IRL[1]	FRA LUX[3]
Rental income				
Tax treatment of pensions and savings account			FIN	
Employee share acquisition deductions				SWE

Note: Countries in brackets have only announced reforms.

[1] In Ireland, the reduced rate of tax on capital gains is a specific relief available only on disposal of certain assets by entrepreneurs. Countries in brackets have only announced reforms.

[2] In the Netherlands, the tax changes would only apply to Box 2 income.

[3] In Luxembourg, the reform applies to capital gains on immovable property.

Source: OECD Annual Tax Policy Reform Questionnaire.

A few base broadening measures were also introduced, mainly for revenue raising purposes (Table 3.4). In the United Kingdom, the tax-free dividend allowance was reduced from GBP 5 000 to GBP 2 000 from April 2018. In the Netherlands, there will be a phasing out of the income tax exemption for imputed rental value for owner-occupied housing[3] with little or no mortgage interest. However, the revenue raised from this reform will be partly offset by a gradual decrease in the rate of imputed rental income. Sweden raised the taxation of savings in investment savings accounts and in endowment insurance (i.e. a form of private pension insurance). Belgium reduced the tax-free threshold for interest on savings deposits from EUR 1 880 to EUR 960. Belgium has also extended the scope of the 30% withholding tax on income realised through bond investment funds: the withholding tax now applies to investment funds investing more than 10% of their assets in debt claims, instead of 25% previously.

On the other hand, some countries have lowered the tax burden on personal capital income

France introduced a flat rate of 30% on capital income, including interest, dividends and capital gains. The new flat tax is comprised of a 12.8% income tax component and a 17.2% social contribution component. This is a significant reform which effectively turns the French PIT system into a dual income tax system as, until 1 January 2018, dividends, interest, and capital gains on the sale of shares earned by individuals were subject to the progressive PIT rates as well as SSCs. Overall, this measure – which aims to support investment – significantly reduces the taxation of personal capital income for higher income taxpayers who previously paid taxes on capital income at high marginal PIT rates.

A number of other measures have lowered tax levels on personal capital income with a view to supporting savings and investment. In Latvia, the 2017 reform exempts dividends at the household level from PIT if the CIT has been paid on these dividends. In Belgium, a new withholding tax exemption on dividends up to EUR 640 was introduced. The Netherlands increased its tax-free threshold on savings and investment income (referred to as Box 3 income) from EUR 25 000 to EUR 30 000 in 2018 to alleviate the tax burden on small savers. The imputed return on savings for Box 3 will also be based on more up-to-date yields. In the Slovak Republic, the capital gains on the sale of shares of domestic corporations (if ownership is greater than 10% and held for more than 24 months) are tax-exempt, in order to align the individual with the corporate tax treatment of such gains[4]. Norway introduced a new scheme for tax-favoured individual pension savings and increased the deductibility of pension savings for the self-employed. Luxembourg extended the temporary measure to tax capital gains on immovable property at a quarter (instead of half) of the PIT rate. In Greece, the capital gains tax will be suspended for amounts arising from the sale of immovable property for an additional year (until the end of 2018).

Table 3.4. Changes to personal capital income tax bases introduced in 2017 and 2018

	Base ⇧		Base ⇩	
Of which	**2017**	**2018 or later**	**2017**	**2018 or later**
Dividend or interest income/equity or bond investment	EST	CAN[1] GBR	(GBR)	BEL LVA NLD
Capital gains		BEL	BEL	GRC NLD SVK
Rental income				NLD
Tax treatment of pensions and savings accounts	AUS EST GBR (NLD) ZAF	BEL SWE	AUS CZE EST FIN ISL LUX PRT	NOR
Employee share acquisition deductions				

Note: Countries in brackets have only announced reforms.

1 In Canada, as a result of reductions in the federal-level small business income tax rate, the "other than eligible" dividend gross up will decrease from 1.17 to 1.16 in 2018 and to 1.15 in 2019. The corresponding dividend tax credit will decrease from 10.5217 per cent to 10.0313 per cent in 2018 and to 9.0301 per cent in 2019.

Source: OECD Annual Tax Policy Reform Questionnaire.

Progress on tax transparency helps countries tax capital income more effectively

In Belgium, the scope of the transparency tax – also known as the "Cayman tax" – has been extended to enhance its effectiveness and close some loopholes. The transparency tax is charged on the income from certain legal constructions, in the hands of Belgian individuals. The 2018 scope extension targets intermediary entities. Distributions made by legal structures without legal personality, such as trusts, are now taxable unless they have already been taxed.

More generally, the global agenda on tax transparency may present opportunities for countries to tax capital income at the household level more comprehensively. The development of Exchange of Information on Request (EOIR) and the introduction of Automatic Exchange of Information (AEOI), which represent a marked change in global tax transparency, are likely to reduce the extent to which taxpayers can evade tax in the future, for example through hiding income offshore. In a recent report, the OECD (2018[3]) has argued that this may present a particular opportunity for countries that previously moved away from progressive taxation of capital income (due to concerns regarding such tax evasion) to reintroduce a degree of progressivity.

Box 3.4. The taxation of household savings

A new OECD report, *Taxation of Household Savings*, provides a detailed review of the taxation of household savings in the OECD and partner countries. The report finds that, while countries do not necessarily need to tax savings more, there is significant scope to improve the way they tax savings. There are opportunities for countries to increase the neutrality of taxation across assets and thereby improve both the efficiency and fairness of their tax systems.

The lack of neutrality in the taxation of savings is illustrated by marginal effective tax rate (METR) modelling undertaken for 40 OECD and key partner countries across a range of potential savings options. The results highlight significant variation in METRs across assets. Private pension funds tend to be the most tax-favoured form of saving, with owner-occupied residential property also significantly tax-favoured. In contrast to owner-occupied residential property, rental property is often subject to relatively high METRs due to the application of progressive marginal personal income tax rates, capital gains taxes and property taxes. Bank accounts and corporate bonds also tend to be relatively heavily taxed in many countries. The report also shows that current tax systems often favour the savings of households that are financially better-off. For example, poorer households tend to hold a significantly greater proportion of their wealth than richer households in bank accounts, which are typically highly-taxed, whereas richer households tend to hold a greater proportion of their wealth in investment funds, pension funds and shares, which are all often taxed relatively lightly.

The report argues that the recent move towards the automatic exchange of financial account information between tax administrations is likely to make it harder in years to come for taxpayers to evade tax by hiding income and wealth offshore – making it less distortive for countries to levy taxes on capital income. This may present a particular opportunity for countries that previously moved away from progressive taxation of capital income (due to concerns regarding such tax evasion) to reintroduce a degree of progressivity. Finally, the report highlights opportunities for equity-enhancing improvements in the design of taxes on household savings. For example, tax deductions provided for private pension contributions and mortgage interest payments could be turned into tax credits so that wealthier taxpayers do not benefit disproportionately from these concessions as compared to poorer taxpayers. Ideally tax credits would be refundable to ensure that taxpayers without sufficient tax liability in a particular year would still receive the full benefit of the tax credit.

Source: (OECD, 2018[3])

Modestly higher employee and employer SSC rates

Broadly, SSC rate changes are evenly split between cuts and increases and base changes are split between broadening and narrowing measures. Compared to previous years, there has been a modest shift in focus towards rate increases and a more significant shift towards SSC base narrowing, particularly for employers and, to a lesser extent, employees. Taken together, the direction of these SSC reforms suggest that in some countries greater contributions will be placed upon a smaller number of contributors. Countries expect these reforms to reduce revenues in the short-term. The stated objectives for undertaking these reforms are wide ranging and include supporting employment and enhancing skills, simplifying the tax system and raising revenues.

There was a mix of modest SSC rate cuts and increases

There were several small SSC rate increases undertaken in 2018 (Table 3.5). In Canada, there were increases to contributions for the Canada Pension Plan (and the Quebec Pension Plan) to take effect in 2019. For amounts below the yearly maximum pensionable earnings (YMPE), there was an increase in the contribution rate of 1 p.p. phased-in over five years. For amounts above the YMPE (but below a new upper limit), there is a new 4% rate starting in 2024. There were also increases in employment insurance premiums for both employees and employers from January 2018 (following decreases in 2017). In Latvia, with the stated objective of supporting healthcare expenditures, the SSC rate will be increased by 1 p.p. from 34.09% to 35.09% in 2018. The employer will now contribute 24.09% and the employee 11%. In addition, the central government solidarity tax will be abolished and replaced by a solidarity payment paid to the SSC budget. In Ireland, there was an increase from 0.7% to 0.8% in employer contributions for the National Training Fund. In Argentina, the employer SSC rate will be progressively increased to 19.5% by 2022.

Table 3.5. Reforms in SSC rates introduced in 2017 and 2018

	Rate ⇧		Rate ⇩	
Of which	**2017**	**2018 or later**	**2017**	**2018 or later**
Employers SSCs	DEU GBR	CAN LAT IRL	(EST) FIN HUN	FRA GER FIN HUN NOR[1]
Employees SSCs	DEU FIN	ARG CAN LAT FIN JYP	LUX	FRA GER JYP
Self-employed			HUN SWE	HUN
Payroll taxes			FRA HUN	

Note: Countries in brackets have only announced reforms.
[1] In Norway, the reform applies to the energy and transport sectors.
Source: OECD Annual Tax Policy Reform Questionnaire.

Some countries made small cuts to SSC rates. In Hungary, the employer social tax rate and health care charge were both reduced from 22% to 19.5% in 2018, following a significant decrease last year from 27% to 22%. The social contribution tax for self-employed workers was reduced by the same amount. In Germany, there were modest decreases in employee health and pension SSCs and also modest decreases in employer pension SSCs. In Norway, differentiated employer SSC rates were introduced in the energy and transport sectors (this is partly offset by abolishing expenditure grant schemes, however).

In some countries, there was a mix of SSC rate increases and decreases in 2018. In France for example, employee SSCs for health and unemployment were reduced with a view to alleviating the tax burden on labour income and enhancing workers' purchasing power. At the same time, the rate of the *Contribution Sociale Généralisée* (CSG), a social levy due on all types of income (including capital and pension income), has been increased by 1.7 percentage points. Another major reform that will come into effect in 2019 is a permanent cut in employer SSC that will replace the existing corporate tax credit for competitiveness and employment (CICE, see section 3.2). In Japan, there was a modest decrease in the employee unemployment contribution but an increase in the rate of employee pension insurance in 2017. In Finland, as part of a negotiated competitiveness pact between the government and trade unions, employer SSCs were decreased while employee SSCs were increased.

Countries have modestly narrowed employer SSC bases

Several base narrowing measures were undertaken (Table 3.6). In Sweden, the Growth Support scheme, which reduces SSCs that employers have to pay for a first employee, was expanded in 2018 to encourage employment. In addition to the aforementioned SSC rate increases in Argentina, there is a monthly exemption of employers SSC for the first ARS 12 000 per employee from 2020 (to be gradually increased from ARS 2 400 in 2018). In 2018, Italy introduced exemptions for employer SSCs targeted at reducing youth unemployment and unemployment in southern regions. However, these exemptions are less generous than the previous exemptions for new permanent contracts that have progressively expired. In the Slovak Republic, new employer and employee SSC allowances for pensioners of EUR 200 were introduced for income from contracts of services in 2018. In Hungary, the health contribution levied on rental income was abolished.

Table 3.6. Reforms in SSC bases introduced in 2017 and 2018

	Base ⇧		Base ⇩	
Of which	**2017**	**2018 or later**	**2017**	**2018 or later**
Employers SSCs	ESP GBR SVK	LAT SVK[1]	POL	ARG HUN ITA SVK SWE
Employees SSCs	ESP GBR SVK	LAT SWE	POL	AUS SVK
Self-employed	ESP GRC	GRC	(FRA) GBR	
Payroll taxes				

Note: Countries in brackets have only announced reforms.
[1] In the Slovak Republic, the health insurance contribution allowance for employers was abolished.
Source: OECD Annual Tax Policy Reform Questionnaire.

There were also a number of base broadening measures. In Latvia, the maximum SSC base will increase from EUR 52 400 to EUR 55 000 and SSC pension contributions will now be levied on royalty income at a rate of 5%. In Australia, the Skilling Australians Fund levy was introduced in March 2018, which charges a levy on businesses that employ foreign workers on certain visas. In the Slovak Republic, the health insurance contribution allowance of EUR 380 for employers was abolished. In Greece, with the objective of raising revenues, self-employed SSCs will be calculated at 85% of an amended taxable income base. In Japan, the long-term care levy paid by medical insurers has been recalculated based on income levels from August 2017 and the changes in the base will be phased in over a three-year period.

Corporate income taxes and other corporate taxes

This section focuses on corporate income tax (CIT) reforms and confirms that CIT rate cuts have accelerated. Compared to previous years, the acceleration in CIT rate cuts has been driven by rate reductions in a number of large economies, including countries with traditionally high corporate tax rates. Other notable reforms have aimed at supporting investment, including the expansion of general investment incentives. Compared to previous years, however, very limited changes have been made to R&D and innovation related tax incentives.

In parallel, many countries have continued to broaden their corporate tax bases both domestically and internationally, although efforts have differed across countries. For instance, in some countries, CIT rate cuts have been accompanied by significant base broadening efforts, while in others they have not. The taxation of highly digitalised businesses has also become a major concern for many countries, but wide disparities in views across countries have prevented the adoption of a common approach so far.

CIT revenues are beginning to pick up again in a number of countries

CIT revenues measured as a percentage of GDP peaked just before the onset of the economic crisis. While in most countries they have increased relative to their levels in 2009 and 2010, CIT revenues as a share of GDP in 2016 generally remained below their levels in 2007-08. Average CIT revenues in the OECD stood at around 3.6% of GDP in 2007, fell to 2.7% in 2009 and have fluctuated since then around 2.8%. Interestingly, CIT revenue trends seem to have been little affected by the progressive decline in CIT rates (Figure 3.6).

Figure 3.6. Unweighted average CIT rate and CIT revenues in OECD countries

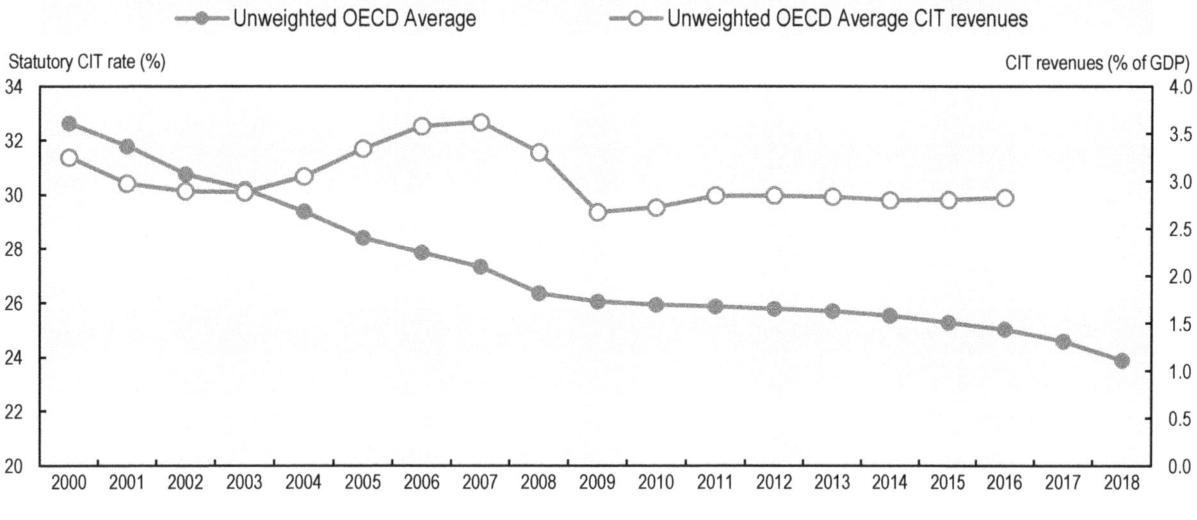

Source: OECD Revenue Statistics and OECD Tax Database.

In recent years, CIT revenues as a share of GDP have picked up in a majority of countries. Figure 3.7 depicts changes in CIT revenues, measured in percentage points of GDP. On average, between 2015 and 2016, CIT revenues increased by 0.06 percentage points in the countries covered in the report. Between 2014 and 2015, the increase was close to zero while revenue changes were negative in the two preceding years. Figure 3.7 shows that the Netherlands, Hungary, the United Kingdom, Mexico, Korea, Germany and Turkey have experienced the strongest increases between 2015 and 2016 with an average of 0.35 percentage points of GDP. On the other hand, Norway, Sweden, Estonia and Argentina have seen significant decreases. Overall, between 2015 and 2016, revenue increases were observed in around three quarters of the countries for which data is available. This evolution in CIT revenues is broadly in line with other macroeconomic indicators discussed in Chapter 1, suggesting that cyclical upturns have contributed to increases in CIT revenues in a number of countries.

Indeed, CIT revenues have been found to be more responsive to the business cycle than other taxes. For instance, Sobel and Holcombe (1996[4]), who proposed a methodology to estimate tax base elasticities with respect to short- and long-term changes in GDP based on US state-level data for 1951 to 1991, found that the CIT base reacts more strongly to short term changes in GDP than PIT, sales or fuel tax bases. However, the PIT base was found to have higher long-term elasticities. More recent studies based on similar methodologies broadly confirm these findings, e.g. for Canadian provinces from 1972 to 2006 (Dahlby and Ferede, 2012[5]) and Latin American countries from 1990 to 2009 (Fricke and Süssmuth, 2014[6]).

Figure 3.7. Changes in CIT revenues in percentage points of GDP

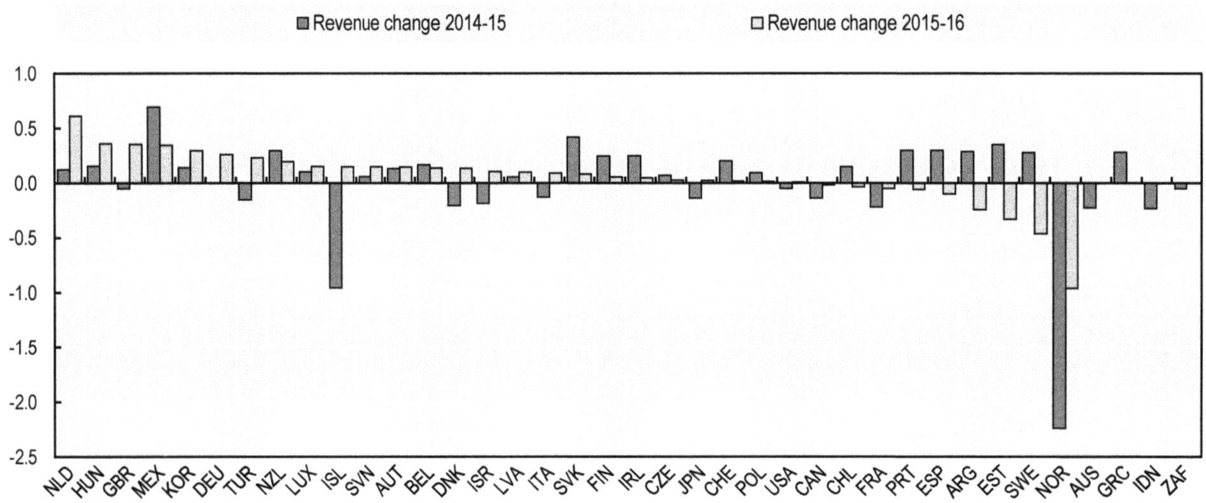

Source: OECD and Global Revenue Statistics databases.

The share of CIT revenues in total tax revenues varies across countries. Figure 3.8 highlights significant regional differences regarding the importance of CIT in countries' tax mixes in 2016. For instance, Indonesia, Chile, Mexico and South Africa had by far the highest shares of CIT revenues in their tax mixes, around 21%. These countries were followed by Asian and Pacific countries including Australia, New Zealand, Korea and Japan, with CIT revenue shares between 12% and 15% of GDP, and several small European countries. Canada, the United States and the United Kingdom had CIT revenue shares of 10.0%, 8.6% and 8.4% respectively, while the corresponding shares in some large European countries were much lower, varying between 6.8% in Spain and 4.5% in France. These regional differences are also likely to reflect regional differences in overall tax-to-GDP ratios (see Chapter 2), with countries with high tax-to-GDP ratios exhibiting lower shares of CIT as a share of total taxation.

Over the last fifteen years, the importance of CIT in countries' tax mixes has generally decreased. Figure 3.8 shows that in all countries except Mexico, the Slovak Republic, Ireland, Iceland and New Zealand, CIT revenue shares were higher in 2007, just before the crisis, than in 2016. Between 2000 and 2016, changes were more mixed. While CIT revenue shares have been relatively constant in Germany and the United States, other large economies, including Japan, Canada, the United Kingdom, France, Italy, Spain, Korea, Australia and Argentina, have experienced reductions in the share of CIT in total tax revenues. On the other hand, some countries have seen large increases in CIT revenue shares, in particular Chile, Mexico and South Africa but also, to a lesser extent, New Zealand and some comparatively small European countries including Iceland, the Slovak Republic, Switzerland, Estonia, Austria and Slovenia.

Various factors can lead to changes in the importance of CIT revenues in the tax mix. As described above, CIT has been found to be more volatile than other taxes and GDP itself. This implies that, during and after an economic downturn, the weight of CIT in total tax revenues may be lower than in a period of economic boom. Additionally, in an open economy, tax competition models predict a shift of taxes from mobile capital to less mobile tax bases such as labour or consumption (Wilson, 1986[7]; Zodrow and Mieszkowski, 1986[8]; Keen and Konrad, 2013[9]). Other factors which can explain changes in the share of CIT in total tax revenues include CIT base broadening and the possible incorporation of businesses to avoid high PIT rates.

Figure 3.8. CIT revenues as a share of total tax revenues

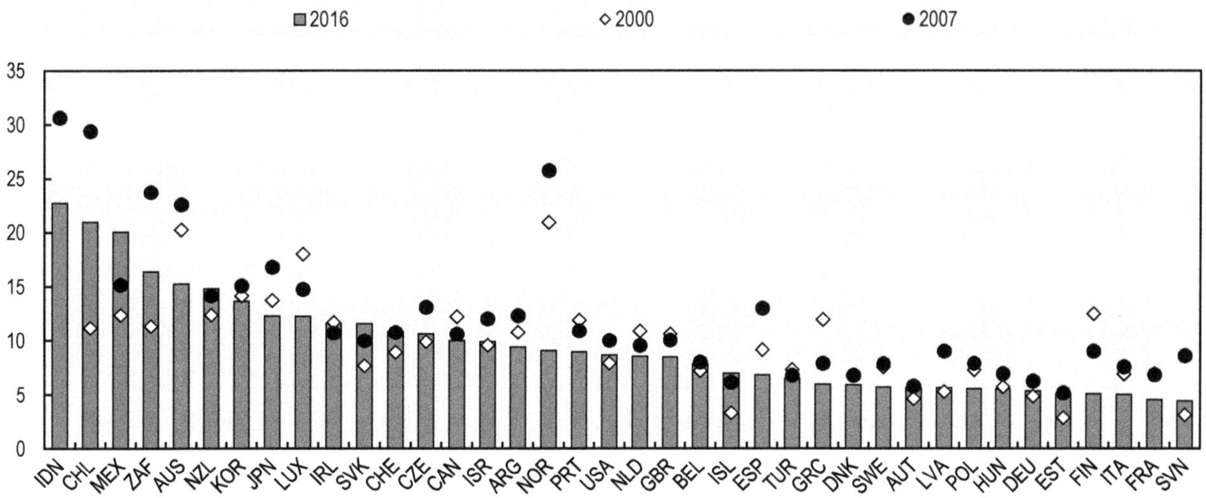

Note: 2015 data used for Australia, Greece, Indonesia, Japan, Mexico and South Africa.
Source: OECD and Global Revenue Statistics databases.

CIT rate cuts have accelerated in 2018

The first observation from countries latest CIT reforms is that CIT rate reductions are continuing. Last year's report noted that eight countries implemented CIT rate cuts in 2017, averaging 2.7 percentage points, and three more had announced similar rate cuts in the coming years. In addition, seven countries had legislated or announced CIT rate reductions for SMEs entering into force in 2017 or later. These trends are continuing. In 2018, eight countries reduced their statutory CIT rates, with an average decrease of around 4.8 percentage points.[5] These countries include Argentina, Belgium, France, Japan, Luxembourg, Norway, Sweden and the United States (Table 3.7).

Among the CIT rate reductions that entered into force in 2018, five were newly legislated. Argentina introduced a gradual rate cut starting with a reduction from 35% to 30% in 2018. A subsequent reduction to 25% has been announced for 2020. As part of a comprehensive corporate tax reform package (see Box 3.5), Belgium reduced its statutory CIT rate from around 34% to 29% in 2018 with the perspective of further reductions to 25% by 2020. France legislated a progressive reduction of the statutory CIT rate from 33.3% to 25% to be phased in gradually between 2018 and 2022. In the first phase of the reform, taking effect in 2018, a reduced rate of 28% will apply only to taxable income up to EUR 500 000; amounts exceeding this threshold will still be taxed at the 33.3% rate. In 2019 a 31% rate will apply above the threshold, while the 28% rate will become universally applicable in 2020. After that date, the rate will be reduced to 26.5% in 2021 and to 25% in 2022. The 3.3% surtax remains unchanged. Sweden reduced its standard CIT rate from 22% to 21.4% in 2019 and 20.6% in 2021.

Box 3.5. Belgium's corporate tax reform package

A comprehensive tax reform package was adopted at the end of 2017, which will be implemented progressively over the 2018-2020 period. As part of the reform, the CIT rate will be progressively reduced. The reform aims to be revenue-neutral by introducing in parallel significant base broadening measures.

More specifically, the CIT rate will be lowered from 33.99% to 25% between 2018 and 2020. The CIT rate for SMEs is also reduced. The participation exemption will be increased from 95% to 100%, while the qualifying requirements for capital gains will be strengthened. The so-called "fairness tax" (an alternative minimum tax) will be eliminated. The main base broadening measures include the transposition of the EU Anti-Tax Avoidance (ATAD I and II) Directives, in particular the implementation of measures relating to CFC rules and interest deduction limitations; the limitation to certain deductions that companies can claim against income through a basket system with a minimum tax base; and the modification of the notional interest deduction. The notional interest deduction will be incremental – i.e. calculated on the equity increase instead of the stock of equity.

The most significant new CIT rate reduction was introduced in the United States. As part of the comprehensive Tax Cuts and Jobs Act (see Box 3.5), the federal CIT rate was cut from 35% to 21%. Assuming an average sub-central CIT rate of around 6%, this reform reduces the combined central and sub-central CIT rate from 38.91% to 25.75%. In addition, the Alternative Minimum Tax (AMT), requiring companies to calculate their tax liability under both the standard CIT and under the AMT rules and to pay the higher of the two, was repealed.

A number of the CIT rate cuts that entered into force in 2018 were part of previously legislated multi-year CIT rate reductions. As announced last year, following a CIT rate reduction from 21% to 19% in 2017, Luxembourg further reduced its statutory CIT rate to 18% in 2018. Norway reduced its statutory CIT rate from 24% to 23%, following a CIT reduction from 25% to 24% last year. In Japan, the national CIT rate was progressively reduced from 25.5% in 2014 to 23.2% in 2018.

Table 3.7. Changes to corporate income tax rates

	Rate ⇧		Rate ⇩	
Into effect in	2017	2018 or later	2017	2018 or later
Standard CIT rate	SVN	CAN[1] KOR[2] PRT[3] TUR	GBR HUN ISR ITA JPN LUX NOR SVK	(AUS) ARG BEL LVA[4] FRA (GBR) (GRE) JPN LUX NOR SWE USA
SME CIT rate			CAN HUN LUX NLD POL POR	BEL CAN
Patent box rate		NLD		

Note: Countries in brackets have only announced reforms.
[1] Several Canadian States changed their general CIT rate in 2018; Quebec reduced its rate from 11.8% to 11.7%, British Columbia increased its rate from 11% to 12% and Saskatchewan increased its rate from 11.5% to 12%; as a result, the weighted average sub-central general CIT tax rate is estimated to have increased to 11.8% in 2018.
[2] Korea increased the CIT rate applicable to companies in the highest bracket, i.e., with taxable bases exceeding KRW 300 000.
[3] Portugal legislated an increase in the State Surtax applicable to companies with more than EUR 35 million of taxable income.
[4] Latvia adopted a new corporate tax regime replacing its business income tax, levied on corporate profits at 15%, with a 20% tax on profit distributions.
Source: OECD Annual Tax Policy Reform Questionnaire.

Finally, some countries announced CIT rate cuts in the future. In the United Kingdom, the CIT rate is scheduled to be reduced to 17% in 2020. Australia has announced a gradual CIT rate reduction to 25% by the 2026-27 fiscal year. Greece announced a CIT rate cut from 29% to 26% which, conditional upon a budget evaluation by the IMF, the European Commission, the European Central Bank, the European Stability Mechanism and the Greek authorities, would take effect in 2020.

In addition to general CIT rate cuts, CIT rates for SMEs have been reduced in two countries. Several Canadian provinces have reduced their SME-specific rates. In Belgium, for SMEs, the CIT rate on the first bracket of EUR 100 000 of net taxable income is reduced to 20.4% (including the crisis contribution) in 2018 and then 20% (with the elimination of the crisis contribution) as from 2020. This SME rate will only apply if a minimum salary of at least EUR 45 000 is paid to the company director.

On the other hand, a few countries have increased CIT rates. Turkey raised its general CIT rate, from 20% to 22%. Latvia adopted a new corporate tax regime replacing its 15% CIT on corporate profits with a rate of 20% on profit distributions, but CIT will no longer be payable on retained earnings. In Canada, several provinces have changed their CIT rates in 2018. Quebec reduced its rate from 11.8% to 11.7%, British Columbia increased its rate from 11% to 12% and Saskatchewan increased its rate from 11.5% to 12%. As a result, the weighted average sub-central Canadian CIT rate is estimated to have increased by 0.1 percentage points to 11.8% in 2018. Portugal raised the state surtax applicable to companies with taxable income exceeding EUR 35 million from 7% to 9%. Korea increased the top CIT rate from 22% to 25%, i.e. for taxable bases exceeding KRW 300 billion. Finally, the Netherlands has increased the rate applicable to income from intangible assets from 5% to 7%.

Overall, combined (i.e. national and sub-national) statutory CIT rates currently range from 9% in Hungary to 34.43% in France (Figure 3.9). While there is variation between countries' CIT rate levels, the move towards lower CIT rates has occurred everywhere, with the exception of Chile which is the only country where the combined CIT rate has increased between 2000 and 2018. Overall, 22 of the 38 countries covered in the report now have combined statutory CIT rates equal to or below 25%, against only six in 2000.

Figure 3.9. Top statutory CIT rates in 2000, 2017 and 2018

Combined (national and sub-national) CIT rates

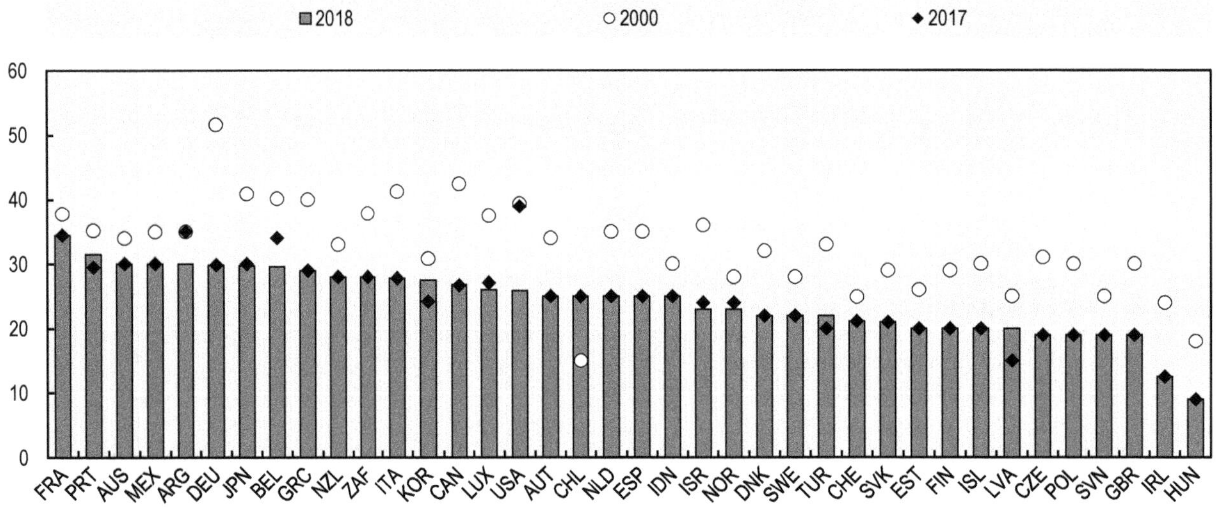

Note: CIT rates updated in June 2018. For France, the 33.3% central statutory CIT rate is used for 2018.
Source: OECD Tax Database and OECD Tax Policy Reform Questionnaire.

Figure 3.9, Figure 3.10 and Figure 3.11 confirm that CIT rate cuts have accelerated in the last few years. CIT rates have declined since 2000 but three phases can be distinguished. CIT rates fell sharply in the years leading to the crisis, with a fall of 6.7 percentage points in the OECD average CIT rate between 2000 and 2008. The OECD average CIT rate then stabilised in the years following the crisis, with a decrease in the OECD average CIT rate of 0.75 percentage points between 2008 and 2015. Finally, between 2015 and 2018, the OECD average CIT rate fell by more than one percentage point, reflecting an acceleration in CIT rate reductions (Figure 3.10). Overall, the OECD average CIT rate dropped from 32.5% in 2000 to 23.9% in 2018. The OECD median CIT rate followed a broadly similar evolution (Figure 3.11).

In 2018, the acceleration in CIT rate cuts has been led by CIT rate reductions in countries with historically high CIT rates. The recent acceleration in CIT rate cuts has to a large extent been driven by CIT rate cuts in countries with traditionally high CIT rates (Figure 3.9), which also tend to be larger economies (e.g. France and the United States which are members of the G7 and caused a drop in the average G7 rate, Figure 3.10). The last two years have also seen a narrowing of the spread of CIT rates across countries. As shown in Figure 3.11, however, the spread of CIT rates across countries has stayed roughly similar, with an approximately constant difference between the maximum and the minimum CIT rates as well as in the interquartile range of CIT rates (i.e. between the 25th and the 75th percentiles).

Figure 3.10. Average CIT rates in OECD G7 and non-G7 countries

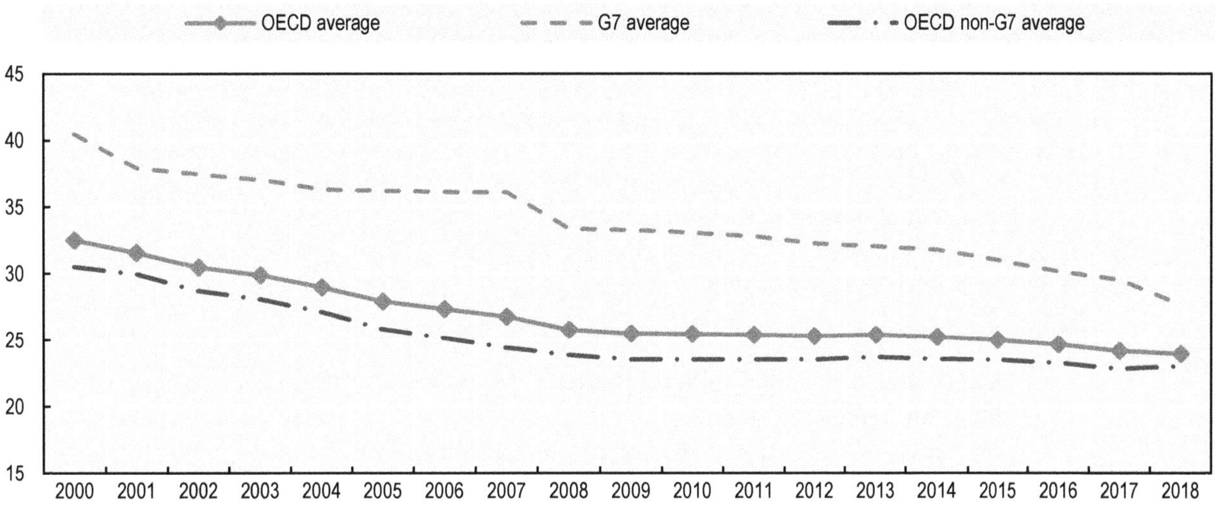

Source: OECD Tax Database and OECD Tax Policy Reform Questionnaire.

Figure 3.11. Range of statutory CIT rates over time

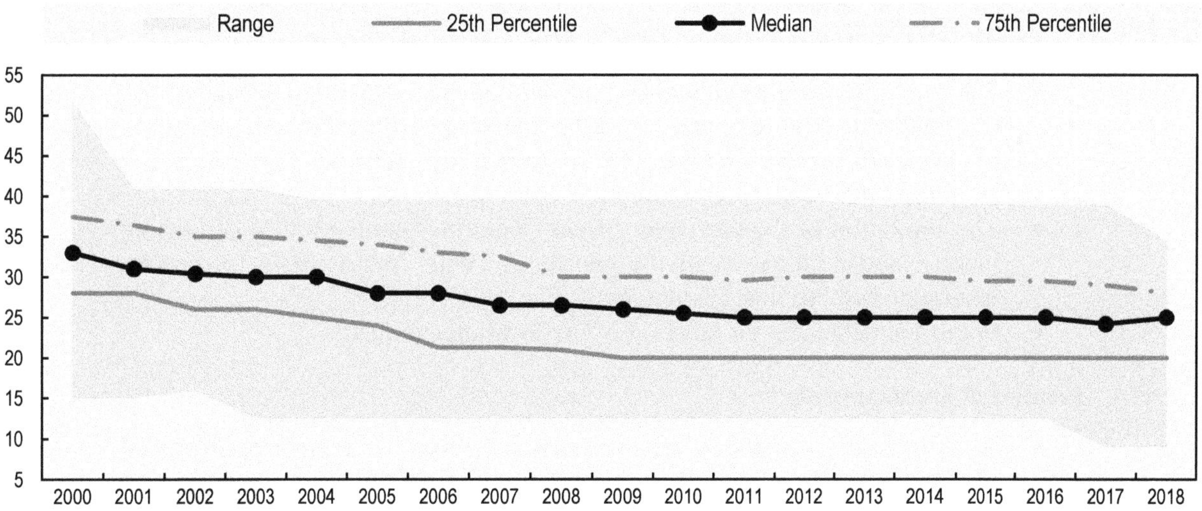

Source: OECD Tax Database and OECD Tax Policy Reform Questionnaire.

Box 3.6. The US Tax Cuts and Jobs Act

The United States President signed the tax reform bill into law on 22 December 2017. This package of measures is considered the biggest overhaul of the US tax system in more than thirty years. It includes substantial corporate and individual tax changes, providing an estimated net tax reduction of approximately USD 1.5 trillion over 10 years according to the Joint Committee on Taxation (not taking into account dynamic effects).

Key domestic corporate tax changes

A number of measures will lower the tax burden on businesses:

- A permanent reduction in the statutory corporation tax rate to 21%, taking effect on 1 January 2018.
- The repeal of the corporate alternative minimum tax.
- Full and immediate expensing of capital investment. The 100% bonus depreciation rule applies through 2022, and then gradually phases down over the succeeding five years.
- A temporary 20% deduction against qualifying business income earned by pass-through entities (i.e. certain partnerships, S corporations and sole proprietorships).

A number of measures are intended to raise revenues, in particular:

- The limitation of the deductibility of net business interest expense to 30% of adjusted taxable income. The new law starts with a broader definition of adjusted taxable income, but significantly narrows that definition beginning in 2022.
- The limitation of the carryover of net operating losses to 80% of taxable income and elimination of the carryback (with special rules for certain insurance and farming businesses).
- Significant changes for taxation of the insurance industry.

Taxation of multinationals:

- A shift from worldwide taxation with deferral to a hybrid territorial regime, featuring a participation exemption regime with current taxation of certain foreign income.
- A reduced effective tax rate for foreign-derived intangible income of US corporations (FDII).
- A minimum tax on the global intangible low-taxed income (GILTI) earned by its foreign subsidiaries, which is the amount of income of a foreign subsidiary that exceeds an implied 10% rate of return on its tangible business assets.
- A minimum base erosion anti-abuse tax (BEAT): a 5% tax (increased to 10% in 2019 and to 12.5% in 2026) calculated on a modified tax base that excludes deductions for payments made to a related foreign party. The tax applies to corporations with average US annual gross receipts of at least USD 500 million, when at least 3% of whose deductions are derived from

Box 3.6. The US Tax Cuts and Jobs Act
(continued)

payments made to a related foreign party.

Individual provisions – subject to sunset in 2025:

The US tax reform also introduced many changes affecting individual taxpayers. Most of those changes (including the deduction for certain owners of pass-through businesses) are scheduled to cease to apply after 31 December 2025, and to revert to their pre-2018 form. Future legislation would be required to make the provisions effective beyond 2025. The main changes that were introduced include:

- Change in the personal income tax rate scale. The new rates are 10%, 12%, 22%, 24%, 32%, 35%, and 37%. The top rate applies to single filers with income over USD 500 000 and married joint filers with income over USD 600 000.
- Near doubling of the standard deduction, with these deductions indexed annually. At the same time, the deduction for personal exemptions is repealed.
- Expansion of the child tax credit and substantial increase in the phase-out thresholds.
- Reduction or elimination of a number of tax preferences, many of them significant and long-standing, including capping the home mortgage interest deduction to interest expenses attributable to mortgage balances no greater than USD 750 000, the elimination of deductions for home equity loan interest, and, most significantly, capping the deduction for state and local taxes at USD 10 000.
- Increase in the alternative minimum tax exemption.
- Doubling of the estate and gift tax exemption to USD 10 million (indexed for inflation) through 2025.

Other major CIT reforms have been introduced to encourage investment

While CIT rate cuts are a highly visible way of enhancing the investment-friendliness of corporate tax systems, other significant reforms have been introduced with that objective. The most notable reforms have included the United States' move from a worldwide to a (hybrid) territorial tax system, the deferral of CIT to the moment profits are distributed in Latvia, as well as the expansion of corporate tax incentives in a few countries.

The United States has moved towards a (hydrid) territorial tax system, following a more global trend

Many OECD countries have shifted away from residence-based or worldwide systems to territorial tax systems for the taxation of foreign corporate profits. For example, the United Kingdom, Japan and New Zealand changed their worldwide systems to a territorial one in 2009. There are various rationales behind a shift to territoriality. First, a territorial system increases the competitiveness of domestically headquartered multinational enterprises (MNEs) which will face the same tax burden as other competitors in a foreign market and therefore reduces the incentive to relocate the headquarters to a lower taxed jurisdiction. Second, the territorial system does not discourage companies from repatriating foreign earnings ("lock-out" effect).

Participation exemptions allow MNEs to exclude profits received from foreign subsidiaries from their domestic tax bases. As Table 3.8 shows, most OECD countries provide participation exemptions close to 100% for dividends and capital gains. In some countries these exemptions are limited to specific groups of countries. Countries with territorial tax systems typically also adopt controlled foreign corporation (CFC) rules and interest deduction limitations in order to discourage domestically headquartered MNEs from eroding the domestic tax base by shifting profits to foreign subsidiaries and then repatriating them at little or no cost.

The US tax reform has shifted corporate taxation from a worldwide to a hybrid territorial system. More specifically, the reform has introduced a 100% deduction for dividends received by US domestic corporations from foreign corporations when they have an ownership stake of at least 10%. No foreign tax credit is allowed with respect to the income generating the dividend. As discussed further, these changes are combined with new international tax provisions implying that certain types of foreign earned income are now taxable in the United States (cf. the GILTI and the BEAT measures). The new regime applies to distributions made after 31 December 2017. The transition to the dividend exemption system is ensured by taxing post-1986 deferred accumulated foreign income. The rates applied are 15.5% for liquid assets and 8% for illiquid ones.

Another important reform was the introduction of a full participation exemption regime in Belgium. In 2018, the Belgian dividend exemption rate was raised from 95% to 100% and the minimum tax of 0.412% on capital gains of large companies was abolished, implying that foreign dividends and capital gains have a symmetric treatment and are now both fully exempted.

Table 3.8. Participation exemptions in 2018

	Foreign Dividend Income Exempted (%)	Foreign Capital Gains Income Exempted (%)	Country Limitations
Argentina	0	0	-
Australia	100	100	None
Austria	100	100	EU / EEA
Belgium	100	100	None
Canada	100	50	Treaty Countries
Switzerland	100	100	None
Chile	0	0	-
Czech Republic	100	100	EU / EEA / Treaty Countries
Germany	95	95	None
Denmark	100	100	EU / EEA / Treaty Countries
Spain	100	100	EU
Estonia	100	100	EU / EEA / Switzerland
Finland	100	100	EU / EEA / Treaty Countries
France	95	88	Blacklist excluded
United Kingdom	100	100	None
Greece	100	0	EU
Hungary	100	100	None
Indonesia	0	0	-
Ireland	0	100	EU / Treaty Countries
Iceland	100	100	None
Israel	0	0	-
Italy	95	95	Blacklist excluded
Japan	95	0	None
Korea	0	0	-
Luxembourg	100	100	None
Latvia	100	100	Blacklist excluded
Mexico	0	0	-
Netherlands	100	100	None
Norway	97	100	EEA
New Zealand	100	100	None
Poland	100	0	EU / EEA / Switzerland
Portugal	100	100	Blacklist excluded
South Africa	100	100	None
Slovak Republic	100	0	Treaty Countries
Slovenia	95	47.5	EU / Blacklist excluded
Sweden	100	100	None
Turkey	100	100	None
United States	*100*	0	None

Note: In most countries, minimum ownership qualifications need to be fulfilled in order to apply the participation exemption. Some countries have anti-abuse provisions.
Source: (Pomerleau and Jahnsen, 2017[10]).

Reforms were introduced to encourage the reinvestment of profits

Raising the price of dividend distributions relative to retained earnings may be used as a way to encourage firms to reinvest their profits. Argentina and Latvia have done so by substantially lowering the cost of capital for investment financed by retained earnings and raising taxes on profit distributions.

Latvia has adopted a new corporate tax regime, replacing its CIT which was previously levied on corporate profits at 15%. As of 1 January 2018, profit distributions and deemed distributions[6] by resident companies and Latvian permanent establishments (PEs) will be taxed at a 20% rate applied to the grossed up amount of profit distributed, which implies that distributed profits are effectively taxed at a rate of 25%.[7] However, CIT will not be payable on retained earnings.[8] Domestic and foreign dividends received will be deductible from the corporate tax base, subject to certain anti-avoidance provisions. Since the tax on distributed profits is not considered to be a dividend withholding tax, the tax rate is not affected by applicable tax treaties. As a transition, distributions made out of retained earnings that have accrued before 2018 will be exempt from the new CIT but taxed at a rate of 10% at the level of the recipient.

In Argentina, the reduction in the statutory CIT rate mentioned above is coupled with the introduction of an additional withholding tax on dividends distributed to resident individuals and non-residents. Initially, the withholding tax rate on dividends is set at 7% for the years 2018-19. However, in line with the announced reduction of the statutory CIT rate to 25% in 2020, the withholding tax rate is scheduled to increase, at the same time, to 13%. This reform is aimed at encouraging the reinvestment of corporate profits.

The Netherlands has increased the scope of its dividend withholding tax exemption

The Netherlands has expanded the scope of the dividend withholding tax exemption. Until 2018, dividend tax did not have to be withheld if the recipient was a member of the EU or the European Economic Association (EEA). As of 2018, the exemption from dividend withholding tax was expanded to third countries that have concluded a tax treaty with the Netherlands that contains qualifying provisions relating to dividend withholding taxes. This implies that outgoing dividend payments are exempt from withholding taxes in situations where a treaty exists.[9] However, the Netherlands has announced the introduction of a withholding tax on outgoing dividends in situations of abuse or in cases of distributions to low-tax jurisdictions, which should become effective in 2020. This provision would also apply to interest and royalty payments as of 2021.

Additionally, it has been proposed to align the treatment of Dutch holding cooperatives with that of public and private limited liability companies. As a result Dutch holding cooperatives are in principle also obliged to withhold a 15% dividend withholding tax on dividend payments.

Several countries have expanded general investment incentives; fewer reforms have been targeted at R&D and environmentally-related investments

A number of tax incentives have been expanded, with a view to supporting investment. These have included in particular the expansion of general investment incentives, changes to depreciation rules and increases in SME-related deductions. In contrast to last year, reforms aimed at supporting R&D and environmentally-friendly investments have been limited (Table 3.9).

Table 3.9. Changes to corporate income tax bases

	Base ⇧		Base ⇩	
Into effect in	2017	2018 or later	2017	2018 or later
Capital allowances and general incentives	NOR	GBR IRL	HUN LUX MEX TUR	ARG DEU DNK HUN LUX USA
Loss carryover provisions	ESP JPN LAT LUX PRT GBR	NLD SWE USA		
SME-related tax base changes			AUS POL PRT TUR	CAN PRT USA
R&D tax incentives and patent box regimes	TUR	USA	MEX	SVK USA
Anti-avoidance measures	AUS BEL GBR NLD	ARG IDN JPN NZL POL SVN USA		
Environmentally-related tax incentives			HUN MEX	LUX
Interest deductions and debt bias	NLD GBR SWE	ARG EST ITA NLD NZL POL SWE USA		

Source: OECD Annual Tax Policy Reform Questionnaire.

The United States has introduced full and immediate expensing of capital investment. The first year bonus depreciation was increased from 50% to 100%, thus introducing the expensing of investments in equipment with tax lives of 20 years or less. This implies that corporate taxpayers can now fully and immediately expense 100% of the cost of qualifying business assets[10] acquired and placed in service after 27 September 2017 and before 1 January 2023. From 2023 to 2027 the bonus depreciation percentage will be decreased by 20 percentage points each year going from 80% in 2023 to zero in 2027, implying that at this date standard depreciation rules will again be applicable.

Argentina introduced a new regime for the revaluation of assets for tax purposes. The new regime aims to address distortions caused by inflation in taxpayers' financial statements. It gives taxpayers the possibility to adjust the value of their assets by applying a "revaluation factor," specified in the law, to the remaining (i.e. not yet depreciated) value for tax purposes of the asset's acquisition or construction cost. While the measure narrows the CIT base, the taxpayers opting for this regime will be subject to a one-time special tax on the amount of the revaluation, with tax rates depending on the revalued assets.

Other changes to general tax incentives and capital allowances were introduced. In Luxembourg, the scope of the general investment tax credit has been expanded; it now also includes the purchase of software as well as electric or hydrogen-fuelled vehicles. Similarly, Hungary has increased the range of eligible investments to be considered for the investment tax incentive.[11] Germany increased the value limit for full and immediate expensing of low-value assets.

Japan has announced new tax incentives with the goal of encouraging companies to increase their employees' salaries. The proposal would introduce a temporary tax credit of 15% of the wage increase with respect to the previous year; this percentage is increased to 20% for large companies investing at least 20% more in employee education and training compared to the average of the previous two years. The tax credit would be available over the next three years to Japanese companies satisfying the following two conditions. First, an increase by at least 3% in the salaries of continuous employees compared to the previous year is required. Second, investment in domestic facilities needs to be at least 90% of the current depreciable basis. SMEs increasing the salaries of continuous employees by at least 1.5% are eligible for a 15% tax credit; the credit is increased to 25% for SMEs increasing the salaries of continuous employees by at least 2.5% and, spending at least 10% more in employee education and training, compared to the previous year.

Very limited changes were made to R&D tax provisions. The United States amended its rules for R&D expenditures. As of January 2022, specified R&D expenditures will have to be capitalised and amortised over five years (or over 15 years for expenditures related to foreign research). Taken in isolation, these changes are expected to broaden the tax base because the option to deduct R&D expenditures as current expenses will no longer be available. With a change going in the opposite direction, the Slovak Republic increased its super-deduction for R&D expenditures from 25% to 100%, implying that related investments can now be fully and immediately expensed.

Mexico and Turkey have expanded tax incentives in Special Economic Zones (SEZs). For some of its SEZs,[12] Mexico has introduced a 100% CIT exemption for the first ten years, reduced to 50% in the following five years. In addition, Mexico grants a 25% deduction for workforce training expenses and a 50% tax credit for employer health and maternity insurance in the first ten years, reduced to 25% in the following five years. Investments in one of the SEZs[13] now benefit from full and immediate expensing of acquisition costs in the first eight years, a 50% deduction for work force training expenses and a 30% tax credit for R&D related expenditures. All these measures took effect in late 2017. In Turkey, buildings located in SEZs are now exempt from property tax.

Denmark passed several provisions related to the extraction of oil and gas in the North Sea. The North Sea Agreement introduces an investment window from 2017 to 2025. It implies that the hydrocarbon deduction will be increased over a six-year period from 5% to 6.5% annually; the declining balance depreciation rate for hydrocarbons will be increased from 15% to 20%; both deductions are now due when tax payments are made rather than at the time of the installation. In addition, a new investment pool of DKK 100 million will be set up for green initiatives related to oil and gas extraction and companies have agreed to pay back the tax discount when oil prices have risen to at least USD 75 per barrel.

Base broadening efforts have continued, both domestically and internationally

A significant number of base broadening reforms have been introduced. The main base broadening reforms have focused on anti-avoidance and the implementation of base erosion and profit shifting (BEPS) counter-measures as well as on additional restrictions to loss carryover provisions (Table 3.9). Among the countries that have reduced their CIT rates, some have introduced significant base broadening reforms to compensate for the revenue losses from CIT rate reductions – in particular Belgium, where the CIT reform is expected to be broadly revenue neutral – while others have not.

Restricting loss-carryover provisions remains a common way to broaden corporate tax bases

Restrictions to loss-carryover provisions remain a common way to broaden corporate tax bases. Apart from anti-avoidance and BEPS-related measures, restrictions to loss carryover provisions have been the most common base broadening measure in 2018. This observation is in line with findings from 2017, when five countries introduced restrictions to loss carryover provisions. In 2018, the Netherlands announced a reduction in the number of years for which losses can be carried forward from nine to six. Similarly, the United States introduced a permanent limit to loss offset deductions of 80% of taxable income which became effective in 2018; while carry-backs are no longer possible, loss offset deductions can now be carried forward not only for 20 years but indefinitely.

While these restrictions aim to maintain CIT revenues, research suggests that they may have considerable efficiency costs arising from the fact that firms are incentivised to invest in less risky and less profitable investments. These effects are likely to increase as firms need time to react to investment incentives delivered by the tax system. Ideally, unlimited carry-backs and carry-forwards should be provided and tax losses should be indexed to inflation to maintain their real value over time. In this case, corporate taxation would be symmetric, removing tax-induced disincentives towards less risky projects and increasing stabilisation effects of corporate taxation. Hanappi (2018[11]) highlights that in 2015 only 18 out of 34 OECD and selected partner economies provided unlimited carry-forwards and most countries did not index tax losses to inflation; in addition, several countries restrict the amount of loss offset that can be obtain in a given fiscal year (see Box 3.6).

Box 3.7. Loss carryover provisions

In modern tax systems, businesses are typically allowed to offset a proportion of their losses against future (loss carry forwards) or past profits (loss carry backs). The OECD has collected data on carryover provisions in 34 OECD and selected partner economies and developed a framework to compare the effects of these rules across countries on the basis of a tax symmetry index. This analysis incorporates country-level information on various carryover provisions such as corporate tax carry-forwards and carry-backs as well as restrictions regarding the timing as well as the amount of losses that can be offset in a given fiscal period.

The following graph shows simulated symmetry measures for stylised investments in machinery and equipment based on country-level corporate tax rules in 2015. If corporate tax systems are fully symmetric, investments with the same pre-tax expected return will also yield equal amounts of post-tax expected returns. For each of the countries depicted on the horizontal axis, the graph shows how tax symmetry varies across a common set of projects with different risk profiles.

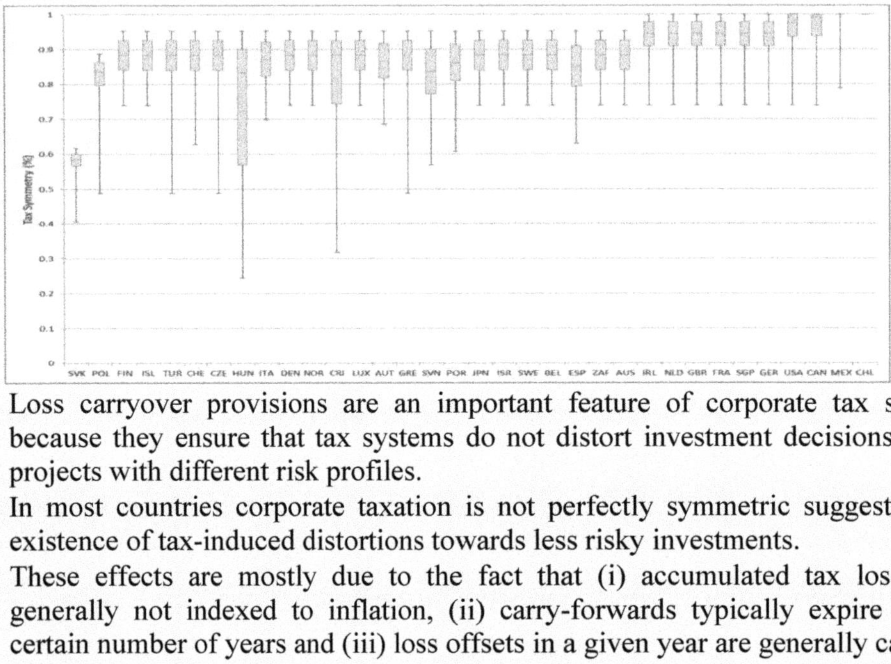

- Loss carryover provisions are an important feature of corporate tax systems because they ensure that tax systems do not distort investment decisions across projects with different risk profiles.
- In most countries corporate taxation is not perfectly symmetric suggesting the existence of tax-induced distortions towards less risky investments.
- These effects are mostly due to the fact that (i) accumulated tax losses are generally not indexed to inflation, (ii) carry-forwards typically expire after a certain number of years and (iii) loss offsets in a given year are generally capped.
- Addressing these three issues will reduce tax-induced distortions and increase tax symmetry; this is particularly relevant for credit-constrained businesses in temporary loss positions allowing policy makers to align the tax treatment of businesses investing in different types of projects.
- Further increases in tax symmetry will improve the allocation of resources across different projects, thus increasing economic efficiency and potentially contributing to economic growth.

Source: (Hanappi, 2018[11])

Other domestic base broadening measures have been introduced, in particular in Belgium as part of its comprehensive CIT reform. The most relevant provisions first include a change in the calculation of the notional interest deduction used to determine the allowance for corporate equity; it will now be calculated based on the incremental equity over a five year period rather than being based on the total stock of qualifying equity in the previous year. Second, a new minimum tax has been adopted for companies with taxable income exceeding EUR 1 million. For taxable income above this threshold certain deductions will be disallowed, implying that there will be a minimum effective taxable basis. Such deductions include deductions for accumulated tax losses, as well as deductions for dividends received, innovation income or notional interest that have been carried forward into the current fiscal year.

Among other base broadening measures were the changes in tax depreciation rules in Ireland and the United Kingdom. The indexation allowance in the United Kingdom is a tax relief given to corporations allowing them to write off inflation from the value of an asset on which chargeable gains are payable when the asset is sold by the corporation. This indexation allowance is no longer available as of January 2018. Ireland introduced a cap on its capital allowances for intangible assets, limiting the capital allowances on specified intangible assets and deductions for related interest expense that can be claimed every year to 80% of trading income from specified intangible assets.

France decreased the rate of its tax credit aimed at boosting competitiveness and employment (CICE) from 7% to 6%. The CICE is available to all companies; it is computed as a percentage of each company's payroll (excluding wages exceeding two-and-a-half times the French minimum wage) and can be directly deducted from CIT liability. The new rate of 6% will become effective as from January 2018. The tax credit will be abolished and replaced by a permanent employer SSC cut in 2019.

The OECD/G20 BEPS measures are being implemented

The OECD/G20 BEPS package was delivered in October 2015 and countries are carrying out its implementation through the Inclusive Framework on BEPS. The package sets out a variety of measures addressing base erosion and profit shifting: new minimum standards, the revision of existing standards, common approaches that will facilitate the convergence of national practices, and guidance drawing on best practices. To ensure the consistent implementation of the BEPS package across countries, the Inclusive Framework on BEPS was created in 2016 and now brings together over 110 countries.

Peer review processes on the four minimum standards have started. The four minimum standards include measures against harmful tax practices (Action 5), preventing treaty abuse (Action 6), Country-by-Country reporting (Action 13) and improving dispute resolution (Action 14). They were agreed to tackle cases where no action by some jurisdictions would have created negative spill overs (including adverse impacts on competitiveness) on others.

In-depth evaluations have been completed to assess the implementation of BEPS Action 5, covering both the exchange of tax ruling information (with over 11 000 rulings already identified and now being exchanged) and the identification of harmful preferential regimes (with over 160 regimes already reviewed, many of which have already been amended, and with over 90 now in the process of being amended or abolished).

Progress has been achieved on the implementation of Country-by-Country (CbC) reporting (Action 13). Over 60 jurisdictions already have a comprehensive domestic legal framework for CbC reporting in place, with around 55 jurisdictions requiring or permitting the filing of CbC reports in 2016, including the headquarter jurisdictions of

MNE groups above the EUR 750 million revenue threshold and over 1 400 exchange relationships activated.

On BEPS Action 14 dealing with the improvement of mutual agreement procedures (MAP), 21 jurisdictions have already been subject to peer reviews, eight are currently underway, and 43 more have been scheduled through December 2019. Furthermore, jurisdictions began reporting their MAP statistics under the MAP Statistics Reporting Framework and the statistics for the year 2016 have already been published.

BEPS Action 6 requires jurisdictions to prevent the granting of treaty benefits in inappropriate circumstances, which can be implemented by participating in the BEPS multilateral instrument or through bilateral treaties. As many jurisdictions will only ratify the BEPS multilateral instrument or bilateral treaties implementing the minimum standard in 2018, the review of the implementation of the minimum standard on treaty-shopping will only begin in 2018. The terms of reference and methodology for these reviews have already been agreed.

A major step in reducing opportunities for tax avoidance by MNEs will be reached on 1 July 2018 as the Multilateral Convention to Implement Tax Treaty Related Measures to Prevent BEPS (also known as the "BEPS Multilateral Instrument") will enter into force. The entry into force of the MLI required ratification by at least five jurisdictions. On 22 March 2018, Slovenia became the fifth country to ratify the MLI following ratification by Austria, the Isle of Man, Jersey and Poland. The entry into force will bring the BEPS Multilateral Instrument into legal existence in these five jurisdictions and its contents will start to have effect for existing tax treaties as from 2019. With 78 signatory jurisdictions, the BEPS Multilateral Instrument covers over 1 200 bilateral tax treaties that will be updated to implement several of the BEPS measures. More jurisdictions are expected to sign and ratify the instrument in the coming period.

In line with BEPS Action 4, several countries have adopted measures to prevent debt shifting through the use of excessive interest deductions. BEPS Action 4 outlines a common approach based on best practices to prevent debt shifting through the use of excessive interest deductions. The Anti-Tax Avoidance Directive (ATAD1), published by the European Commission in 2016, builds on the BEPS recommendations on Action 4 and includes, among other anti-avoidance measures, interest limitations on debt from related and unrelated parties to discourage artificial debt arrangements. Following the BEPS Action 4 recommendations, a number of countries have introduced or announced changes to their interest limitation rules including Argentina, Belgium, Finland, Italy, the Netherlands, New Zealand, Poland, Sweden and the United States.

The United States introduced new measures that will significantly affect the taxation of MNEs

As part of its tax reform, the United States introduced additional measures that will significantly affect the taxation of MNEs. First, Global Intangible Low Taxed Income (GILTI), defined as excess income over a 10% rate of routine return on tangible assets, earned by Controlled Foreign Corporations[14] (CFCs) must now be included as income by US shareholders in a manner similar to subpart F income.[15] However, if the shareholder is a C-corporation, a 50% deduction can be claimed against the shareholder's CIT tax base.[16] Moreover, if the corporate shareholder has been subject to foreign taxation, a foreign tax credit of 80% will be granted. Taken together, these provisions imply[17] that no residual tax is owed by a domestic US corporation with respect to GILTI if the foreign tax rate on the same income is 13.125% or higher. While the aforementioned participation exemption for dividends makes the US tax system more territorial, the GILTI provision implies that certain foreign earned income becomes taxable in the United States with the objective of limiting tax avoidance.

In parallel, there will be a new deduction for foreign derived intangible income. The measure introduces a deduction of 37.5% (21.875% after 2025) for Foreign Derived Intangible Income (FDII) earned by a US corporation from foreign sales or services. FDII is computed as the portion of the excess returns over 10% of tangible assets which is attributable to foreign sales. Taking the new statutory CIT rate of 21% and the 37.5% deduction into account, this FDII is subject to an effective tax rate of 13.125% (the effective tax rate will increase to 16.406% when the deduction is reduced to 21.875%). This measure is intended to support firms choosing to export from the United States.

A new Base Erosion and Anti-abuse Tax (BEAT) was also introduced, effectively imposing a minimum tax on certain foreign income. More specifically, the BEAT is a 5% minimum tax (increased to 10% in 2019 and to 12.5% in 2026) imposed on a modified tax base which is calculated by adding base eroding payments back into the regular corporate tax base. Base eroding payments include payments to foreign related parties[18] in connection with the acquisition of depreciable or amortizable property for which a deduction is allowed; they do not include expenditures that reduce gross receipts, such as the cost of goods sold.[19] The BEAT applies to domestic companies and PEs in the United States, which are members of an MNE group, if the group's average annual gross receipts exceed USD 500 million and the share of base eroding payments to total deductions is higher than 3%. Special rules apply to banks and security dealers.

There is an increasing focus on the taxation of highly digitalised businesses

There has also been an increasing focus on the tax challenges arising from digitalisation. Digitalisation has led to the emergence of new business models and these changes have placed pressure on two key principles underlying the international tax system, namely "nexus" and "profit allocation". In March 2018, the OECD released an Interim Report on the *Tax Challenges Arising from Digitalisation* (OECD, 2018[12]). In the Interim Report, a number of salient features were identified that are frequently observed in the business models of some highly digitalised firms: cross-jurisdictional scale without mass, heavy reliance on intangible assets, especially intellectual property (IP) and the importance of data, user participation and their synergies with IP.

The OECD is working towards reaching a long-term multilateral solution to address the tax challenges arising from digitalisation by 2020. As discussed in the Interim Report (OECD, 2018[12]), members of the Inclusive Framework hold different views on the question of whether, and to what extent, the features identified as being frequently observed in certain highly digitalised business models should result in changes to international tax rules. In particular, with respect to data and user participation, there are different views on whether they should be considered as contributing to a firm's value creation, and therefore on the impact they may have on international tax rules. Acknowledging these divergences, countries have agreed to undertake a coherent and concurrent review of the "nexus" and "profit allocation" rules that would consider the impacts of digitalisation on the economy, relating to the principle of aligning profits with underlying economic activities and value creation. It is anticipated that the Inclusive Framework will work towards a consensus-based solution by 2020.

While the Interim Report highlighted the importance of working towards a multilateral solution, it also recognised that some countries believe that there is a strong imperative to act quickly and are in favour of the introduction of interim measures. On the other hand, there is no consensus on the need for, or merits of, interim measures, with a number of countries opposed to such measures on the basis that they will give rise to risks and adverse consequences. In the Interim Report, those countries in favour of implementing interim measures have identified a number of considerations that they believe need to be taken into account to limit the possible adverse side-effects (OECD, 2018[12]).

Some jurisdictions have announced their intention to implement interim measures. Italy, for instance, will introduce a Levy on Digital Transactions, taking effect on 1 January 2019 (see Box 3.7). It is intended to capture economic value, associated with user-generated content, which is currently not part of the corporate tax base. The tax is imposed at a 3% rate on the amounts paid (net of VAT) in exchange for the provision of digital services supplied electronically; a list of taxable transactions will be provided in a forthcoming decree.

Box 3.8. Italy's Levy on Digital Transactions

The Levy on Digital Transactions ("LDT") is a transaction-based tax proposed by the Italian Parliament and adopted in 2017. It applies to both resident and non-resident enterprises and is expected to become effective from 1 January 2019. The stated objective is to restore a level playing field between suppliers of digital services and other suppliers of more "conventional" services, by taxing digital transactions whose value, generated by users and user-generated content, is currently not captured (or at least is only partially captured) by existing corporate tax rules. Some parallels can be drawn with the "Equalisation Levy" described in the BEPS Action 1 Report and the digital services tax on revenues proposed by the European Commission.

The LDT is imposed at a rate of 3% on the "value" of the taxable transactions, i.e., the amount of consideration paid (net of VAT) in exchange for the provision of digital services supplied electronically. The taxable transactions are defined as services delivered over the Internet or an electronic network and the nature of which means that their supply is essentially automated, involves minimal human intervention, and is impossible to complete without information technology. A specific list of taxable transactions will be provided by a forthcoming decree expected to be issued by 30 April 2018.

Focused on the destination of the supplies, the LDT applies only to business-to-business transactions (B2B) concluded with customers resident in Italy (including permanent establishments in Italy of non-resident enterprises), other than certain defined small businesses. In contrast, the place where the transaction is concluded, together with the residence and/or location of the supplier, is irrelevant.

The tax liability rests formally on the supplier of the taxable transactions, irrespective of its location and/or residency. This includes typically domestic and foreign-based online platforms supplying B2B services to Italian customers. An exemption is, however, available for suppliers that contract no more than 3 000 taxable transactions in a calendar year (i.e., minimum activity threshold). In contrast, the responsibility to collect the tax falls on the Italian customer. The latter withholds the tax when the payment for the service is made and remits it to the tax authorities.

Importantly, the LDT is not creditable against any other Italian taxes due by the taxpayer (e.g. CIT, local taxes, wage taxes) and does not cover non-monetary transactions (e.g., online platforms with advertising-based revenue models), B2C transactions, and supplies of goods. Domestic-based suppliers will, however, be able to deduct the tax from their domestic corporate tax base, while deductibility for foreign suppliers will depend upon corporate tax rules of other countries. Designed as a transaction-based tax, it should apply to domestic and foreign-based suppliers of online services irrespective of their level of physical presence in Italy and should fall outside the scope of double tax treaties. The estimated revenue of the LDT is EUR 190 million per year (circa USD 235 per year).

In March 2018, the European Commission proposed changes to the taxation of digitalised businesses through two proposed directives. The first proposed directive lays down rules for the corporate taxation of a significant digital presence in the EU. It describes a set of rules for establishing a taxable nexus for digital businesses whose cross-border activities allow them to have a non-physical commercial presence in a foreign jurisdiction. In addition, the proposal sets out principles for attributing profits to digital businesses in situations where there is a significant digital presence in a foreign jurisdiction. The stated objective of this proposal is to better capture the value creation of digital businesses which rely heavily on data or user participation. The second proposed directive lays down a common tax on revenues resulting from the provision of certain digital services to EU users. This digital services tax is conceived as an interim measure intended to protect national tax bases as well as the integrity of the single market until a long-term solution is adopted. The treaty on the Functioning of the European Union (TFEU) provides for the Council of the European Union, acting unanimously and after consulting the European Parliament and the European Economic and Social Committee, to issue directives. This implies that the proposed directives would need to get unanimous approval by EU member states.

VAT/GST[20] and excise duties

Overall, this section shows that VAT rates have stabilised, but that increased revenues are expected from significant tax administration and anti-fraud measures in a number of countries. South Africa is the only country where the standard VAT rate was raised in 2018. High VAT rates have led many countries to look for alternative ways of raising additional VAT revenues, through base broadening – by removing or scaling back reduced VAT rates – and administrative and anti-fraud measures. Some of these measures, in particular split payments and the expansion of the domestic reverse charge mechanism, imply major changes to the way VAT has traditionally been collected. In some countries, reduced VAT rates have been expanded to address fairness concerns or to support specific industry sectors, although evidence shows that these tend to be poorly targeted policy instruments.

In the area of excise duties, new taxes are being introduced to deter harmful consumption, in addition to continued increases in excise duty rates on tobacco and alcohol. Some of the most notable reforms include new taxes on sugar-sweetened beverages in Ireland, South Africa and the United Kingdom, and the introduction of a tax on cannabis in Canada.

VAT revenues have reached record levels

VAT revenues have increased in a majority of countries in the last fifteen years. Across the countries covered in the report, VAT revenues ranged from 3.4% of GDP in Switzerland to 9.6% of GDP in New Zealand in 2016 (Figure 3.12). Despite these differences in levels of VAT revenues, most countries have seen their VAT revenues increase compared to 2000. Out of the 37 surveyed countries that have a VAT (i.e. all the countries covered in this report except the United States), 27 recorded increases in their VAT revenues as a share of GDP between 2000 and 2016. There were exceptions, however, notably Ireland and Iceland, which saw their VAT revenues as a share of GDP decrease between 2000 and 2016. In Ireland, however, this drop was due to extraordinary GDP growth.

Figure 3.12. VAT revenues as a share of GDP by country

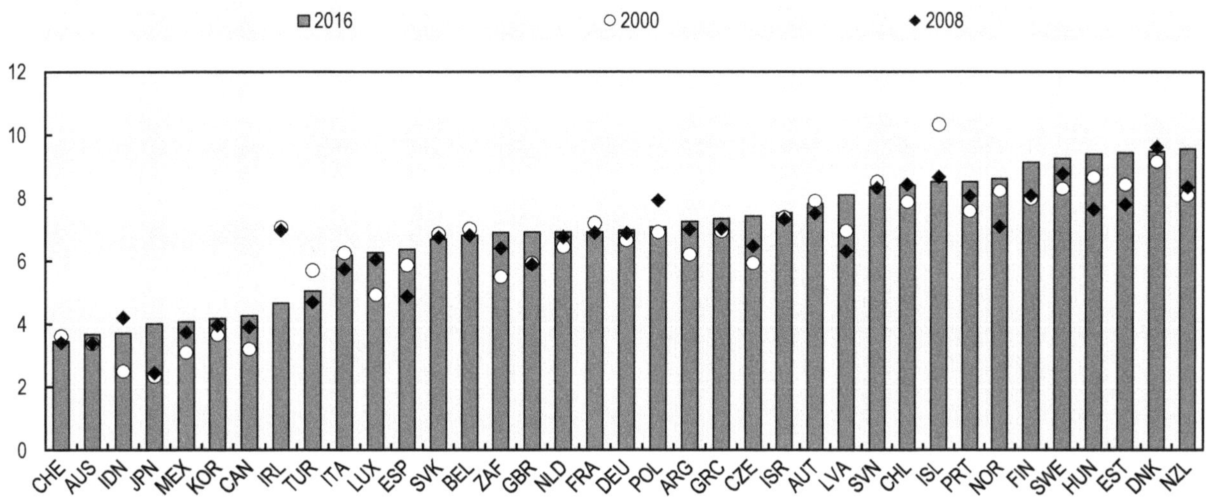

Note: 2015 data for Australia, Greece, Indonesia and South Africa.
Source: OECD and Global Revenue Statistics databases.

Longer-term trends show that VAT revenues have reached historically high levels in most countries. VAT revenues, which used to account for less than 9% of total tax revenues on average in the OECD in 1975, have become the predominant source of consumption tax revenues and now make up on average about one fifth of total tax revenues in the OECD (Figure 3.13). The continuous rise in VAT revenues is the consequence of various factors including the progressive substitution of specific consumption taxes with VAT in most countries and the gradual increases in VAT rates (see below).

As a result, although consumption taxes as a share of GDP have remained stable over the last 30 years, the share of VAT within this category has grown substantially, balanced with the diminishing share of taxes on specific goods and services. Excise taxes and other specific consumption taxes accounted for around 18% of total tax revenues in 1975. Today, they account for less than 10% of the OECD's average tax mix. In Argentina, Indonesia and South Africa, taxes on specific goods and services account for comparatively higher shares of total tax revenues, respectively making up 11.2%, 13.2% and 15.9% of total taxation in 2015.

Figure 3.13. Evolution of the share of consumption tax revenues in total tax revenues in the OECD

OECD average between 1975 and 2015

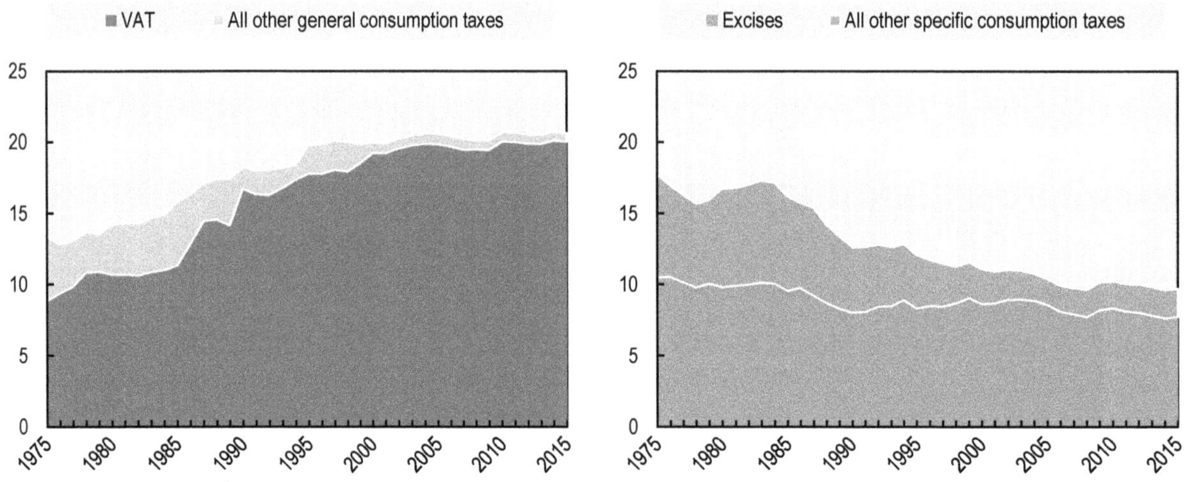

Source: (OECD, 2017[13]), *Revenue Statistics: 1965-2016*, based on OECD Revenue Statistics database.

Standard VAT rates have reached a plateau in recent years

Many countries raised their standard VAT rates after the crisis. Between 2008 and 2015, the OECD average standard VAT rate increased by 1.5 percentage points, from 17.6% to a record level of 19.2%, accelerating a longer term rise in standard VAT rates (Figure 3.14). Standard VAT rates were raised at least once in 23 countries between 2008 and 2018, and 12 countries now have a standard rate of at least 22%, against only six in 2008 (Figure 3.15). Hungary, which has recorded the most significant rate increase since 2008, now has the highest standard VAT rate among the countries covered in the report (27%). Raising standard VAT rates was a common strategy for countries seeking to achieve fiscal consolidation in the wake of the crisis as increasing VAT rates provides immediate revenues without directly impacting competitiveness and has generally been found to be less detrimental to economic growth than raising direct taxes (OECD, 2010[14]).

Figure 3.14. Evolution of the OECD average standard VAT rate until January 2018

Unweighted OECD average VAT/GST rate in %

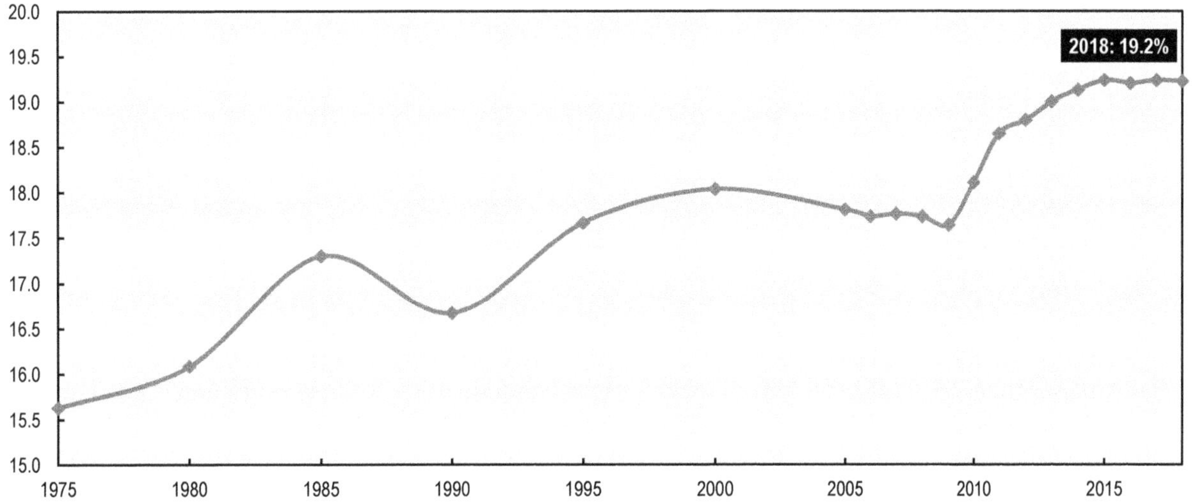

Source: OECD Tax Database.

Figure 3.15. Standard VAT rates by country in 2000, 2008 and 2018

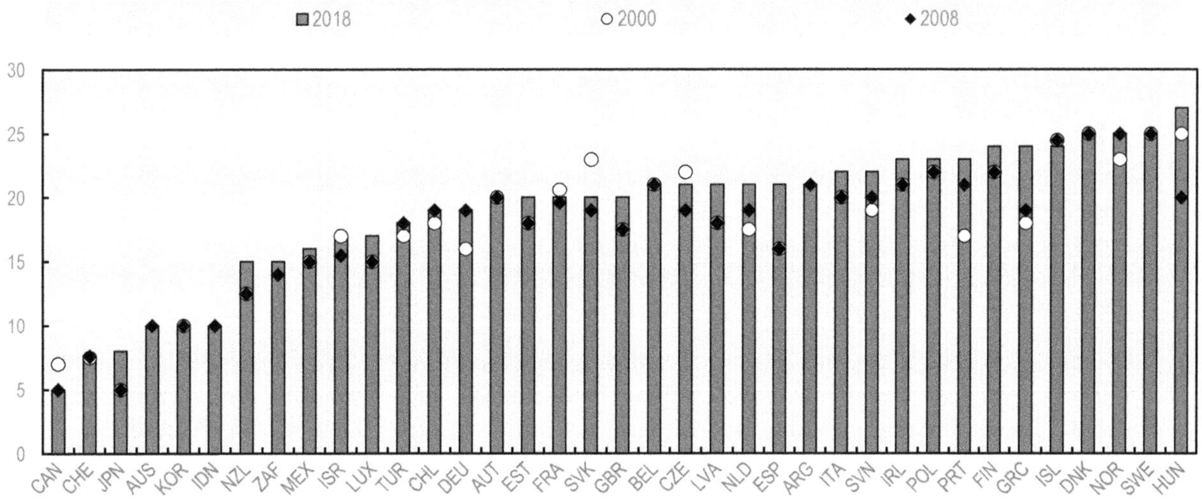

Note: VAT rates updated in June 2018.
Source: OECD Tax Database.

However, the trend towards continuously increasing standard VAT rates has come to a halt in recent years (Figure 3.14). The stabilisation in standard VAT rates is partly explained by the fact that countries are in better fiscal positions (see Chapter 1). Standard VAT rates have also stopped increasing because they have reached high levels in many countries, limiting the potential for additional rate increases.

Only a few countries have announced increases in their standard VAT rates for 2018 and 2019. In its 2018 budget, South Africa announced an increase in its standard VAT rate from 14% to 15% as of 1 April 2018. This standard VAT rate increase – the first in 25 years – is intended to address concerns about the country's growing budget deficit and to compensate for larger than expected tax revenue shortfalls. Japan has signalled its intention to increase its consumption tax rate from 8% to 10% in October 2019. In Italy, the increase in VAT rates for 2018 was postponed. Under the current legislation, if the government fails to implement offsetting measures (spending cuts or alternative tax hikes), the standard VAT rate of 22% will be raised first to 24.2% in 2019 and then to 24.9% in 2020 and 25% in 2021. This suggests that increasing standard VAT rates is still seen by governments as a way to rapidly raise revenue when faced with severe budget constraints. Switzerland was the exception; its standard VAT rate, which had temporarily been raised to 8%, was lowered to 7.7% as of 1 January 2018.[21] Switzerland now has the second lowest standard VAT rate in the OECD (Figure 3.15).

Changes were made to reduced VAT rates, mainly to broaden their scope

Some countries have broadened their VAT bases by increasing reduced VAT rates or by reducing their scope (Table 3.10). Norway raised its reduced VAT rate on cinema tickets, public transportation, hotel accommodation, museums and amusement parks from 10% to 12%, following an increase from 8% to 10% in 2016. The other reduced VAT rate of 15% remains unchanged. In the Netherlands, the government has proposed raising the reduced VAT rate which applies to basic foodstuffs, books, medicine, antiques, entry to museums, swimming pools, zoos, theatre, sports, etc. from 6% to 9% as of 1 January 2019, as part of a broader effort to rebalance the tax mix from direct to indirect taxes. Poland raised its VAT rate from 8% to 23% on a number of specific products (including certain sanitary and pharmaceutical products) and Ireland raised VAT on sunbeds to the standard rate. In Italy, the possible increase in the standard VAT rate would be accompanied by a gradual increase in the 10% reduced VAT rate.

These reforms are broadly in line with OECD findings and recommendations. Maintaining a broad VAT base – through a limited use of reduced VAT rates – minimises distortions and gives countries room to keep standard VAT rates at current levels or to possibly even lower them. In addition, some of the recently introduced reforms have focused on scaling back reduced VAT rates that are typically regressive in the sense that they provided greater benefits to richer households in both aggregate and relative terms (Box 3.8).

On the other hand, a number of countries have lowered VAT rates on foodstuffs for fairness reasons. Latvia introduced a new 5% reduced VAT rate for certain fruit and vegetables. In Hungary, where the standard VAT rate is the highest, the VAT base was further narrowed by expanding the scope of reduced VAT rates. Indeed, following the reduction of VAT for milk, eggs and poultry last year, the 5% reduced VAT rate was extended to pork offal and fish as of 1 January 2018. Argentina reduced its VAT rate for chicken, pig and rabbit meat and Greece reduced the VAT rate on farm intermediate inputs. These reduced VAT rates on food products seek to enhance equity by alleviating the tax burden on the products that form a larger share of poorer households' expenditures. However, recent OECD analysis (see Box 3.8) shows that such reduced rates are not well-targeted as they often end up providing greater benefits in absolute terms to richer households.

Other reduced VAT rates were expanded, often to support specific sectors of the economy. In Hungary, the VAT rate on restaurant services, which was already cut from 27% to 18% in 2017, was further reduced to 5% in 2018 and the reduced VAT rate for internet access services was lowered from 18% to 5%. In Switzerland, e-books are now subject to the reduced VAT rate of 2.5%, instead of the standard rate. Spain cut its VAT rate on live cultural shows. Sweden reduced the VAT rate on the "display" of natural areas to promote tourism. In Greece, the reduced VAT rate for some islands was extended for six months (until 30 June 2018) and the VAT rate for retirement home services was lowered. Austria has also announced a possible cut in the reduced VAT rate on accommodation services from 13% back to its previous level of 10% in November 2018. Some of these VAT rate cuts, in particular those targeting restaurant and accommodation services, are not in line with OECD advice as they tend to be regressive (Box 3.8).

Table 3.10. Changes to reduced VAT/GST rates

	General	Food	Hotels/ Restaurants	Newspapers/e-books	Culture	Other
Rate ⇧ or scope ⇩	(ITA) (NLD) NOR					IRL POL
Rate ⇩ or scope ⇧	LVA	ARG GRC HUN LVA	(AUT)	CHE	ESP	GRC HUN SWE

Note: Countries in brackets have only announced reforms.
Source: OECD Annual Tax Policy Reform Questionnaire.

The European Commission has recently proposed giving EU member states more flexibility in setting their reduced VAT rates. Current rules allow EU member states to have two reduced rates of at least 5%. Recently, however, the European Commission has proposed enabling member states to apply a third reduced rate between 0% and 5%, in addition to the two existing reduced rates and the zero rate. This is intended to address an anomaly whereby some member states have this discretion while others do not. The proposal also includes replacing the current complex list of goods and services to which reduced rates can be applied with a new negative list of products to which reduced or zero rates cannot be applied. To safeguard public revenues, EU member states would have to ensure that the weighted average VAT rate is at least 12%. The proposal will require unanimous agreement from all member states in the Council before it can enter into force (European Commission, 2018[15]).

Box 3.9. The distributional effects of reduced VAT rates in OECD countries

With the exceptions of Chile and Japan, all OECD countries have one or more reduced VAT rates to support various policy objectives. A major reason for the introduction of a differentiated rate structure is the promotion of equity. Countries have generally considered it desirable to alleviate the tax burden on goods and services that form a larger share of expenditure of the poorest households (e.g. basic food, water). Countries also often decide to not tax medicine, health services and housing at high rates. Reduced VAT rates have also been used to stimulate the consumption of "merit" goods (e.g. cultural products and education) and other non-distributional objectives such as promoting locally supplied labour-intensive activities (e.g. tourism) and correcting externalities (e.g. energy-saving appliances).

In general, VAT exemptions, zero-rates and reduced rates are not a well-targeted tool to support low-income households. Reduced rates that are implemented in countries for the distinct purpose of supporting the poor (i.e. to address distributional goals) typically do have the desired progressive effect. For example, reduced rates for basic food provide in general greater support to the poor than the rich as a proportion of household income or expenditure. However, despite this progressive effect, these reduced VAT rates are a very poor tool for targeting support to poor households. At best, rich households receive roughly as much benefit – in absolute value – from a reduced rate as do poor households. At worst, rich households benefit vastly more than poor households. This result is unsurprising as better off households can be expected to consume more, and often more expensive, products than poorer households. Thus, while poorer households may benefit from reduced VAT rates on "necessities" the wealthier gain even more.

Cash transfer programmes that cover the entire population, if well-functioning, are a more effective tool to compensate poor households for the VAT they have paid. If poor households can be compensated directly through a cash transfer programme, it is more efficient and fair to tax all goods and services at the standard VAT rate and compensate the poor directly through cash transfers (and/ or reductions in personal income taxes, etc.), especially if the standard VAT rate is not particularly high. It should immediately be noted, however, that compensating all (and only the) losers of a reform through a transfer programme might in practice be very difficult to achieve.

With regard to preferential VAT provisions for social, cultural and other non-distributional goals, richer households benefit considerably more from VAT exemptions and reduced rates. Those tax provisions often provide so large a benefit to rich households that the reduced VAT rate actually has a regressive effect – benefiting the rich more both in aggregate terms and as a proportion of expenditure. For example, reduced rates on hotel accommodation and restaurant food benefit the rich vastly more than the poor, both in aggregate and proportional terms, in all OECD countries in which they are applied. Similar results, but of less absolute magnitude, are found for reduced rates on books, cinema, theatre and concerts.

Finally, VAT rate differentiation might not be the best policy instrument to correct negative externalities. VAT rate differentiation may improve efficiency if it means that the private marginal costs of an activity are brought closer to the marginal costs for society. However, VAT is a blunt instrument for addressing environmental externalities,

Box 3.9. The distributional effects of reduced VAT rates in OECD countries *(continued)*

as it may be hard to target the actual source of pollution. For example, reduced rates on energy-saving appliances may boost demand or them and therefore stimulate the consumption of these goods. The reduced VAT rate may give incentives to shift from more to less energy-consuming items (consumers might replace their old refrigerator with a new one, for instance). However, this may also lead to an increase in the purchase of energy-intensive products (e.g. consumers may replace their old refrigerator with a new refrigerator and a freezer).

Source: (OECD/KIPF, 2014[16]).

Administrative improvements and anti-fraud measures have been a central part of countries' VAT reforms

A significant number of VAT reforms have revolved around technical and administrative improvements to enhance tax collection and combat fraud. Some of these reforms reinforce taxpayers' reporting obligations, including the use of Standard Audit Files for Tax (SAF-T) and real-time data transfer to tax administrations such as VAT invoice reporting. Other measures modify tax collection mechanisms to combat certain types of VAT fraud. These include split payments and the expansion of the domestic reverse charge mechanism to sectors subject to high risks of fraud. Finally, some of these reforms extend VAT accountability to other entities in the value chain (e.g. online marketplaces). Countries generally expect these measures to bring in significant additional tax revenues.

The adoption of SAF-T is progressing slowly. SAF-T was developed by the OECD (OECD Forum on Tax Administration, 2010[17]) to enable the transfer of accounting data from companies to tax authorities in a standardised electronic format. The main purpose was to allow tax authorities to conduct more efficient tax inspections. The surveyed countries that currently use (a form of) SAF-T include Austria, France (on a voluntary basis), Luxembourg, Poland and Portugal. On 1 January 2018, Poland extended mandatory SAF-T submissions, previously only required from large companies, to all companies. Norway has delayed the introduction of mandatory SAF-T reporting – initially set to enter into force in 2018 – but still plans to implement it by 2020. So far, each country has adopted its specific SAF-T requirements rather than a standard version.

Recent reforms have shown the increasing popularity of real-time VAT invoice reporting. In July 2017, Spain introduced a system of near-live VAT invoice reporting, requiring large taxpayers to electronically report VAT invoices within four days of their issuance. In Hungary, VAT invoice live reporting is set to enter into force from 1 July 2018. It will apply to all business-to-business (B2B) invoices with VAT chargeable above HUF 100 000 (approximately EUR 320) and require customers receiving invoices to report them in real time (within 24 hours) to the tax authorities. In Italy, mandatory real-time electronic invoicing will start progressively in July 2018 and become fully effective in January 2019. The system will require all relevant invoices to be submitted to the Italian Revenue Agency's e-invoicing platform which will verify and approve all taxable transactions in real time. Regarding business-to-consumer (B2C) transactions, Poland is also envisaging the gradual introduction of cash registers that will automatically and in real time transfer information regarding each registered transaction to the Revenue Administration's central digital database.

The use of the domestic reverse charge mechanism is expanding in European countries. The domestic reverse charge mechanism is increasingly being used to combat missing trader fraud in the EU, whereby fraudsters import goods free of VAT, charge VAT when they sell the goods and disappear before remitting VAT to the government.[22] The domestic reverse charge mechanism addresses this type of fraud by making the customer liable to collect the tax on domestic supplies (instead of the supplier), which prevents the supplier from collecting VAT and disappearing with it. This mechanism is increasingly applied by EU member states for goods that are most often used to run such fraud, mainly high-value goods easily transported from one country to another (e.g. mobile phones, laptops, gold, etc.). In this context, Greece recently adopted the domestic reverse charge mechanism for sales of specific electronic devices (mobile phones, gaming consoles, tablets and laptops). In Latvia, as of 1 January 2018, the reverse charge mechanism was extended to supplies of building materials, gaming consoles and household appliances. As part of its efforts to combat the shadow economy, Latvia also lowered its VAT registration threshold from EUR 50 000 to EUR 40 000 and reduced the threshold for disclosing individual invoices from EUR 1 430 to EUR 150.

Split payment is increasingly being considered as an alternative VAT collection method to fight against fraud. Under split payment mechanisms, unlike the standard VAT collection method, the VAT charged by businesses on their supplies is not actually collected by the supplier but collected separately to ensure its payment to the tax authorities. Different split payment methods are being introduced or considered by a few countries. In Poland, split payments will require B2B customers to pay the VAT element of their invoices into a separate VAT bank account held by their suppliers, which will be monitored by the tax authorities and used exclusively to settle suppliers' VAT liabilities. The new system, originally supposed to enter into force in January 2018, will become effective in July. Poland's split payment method is different from the one used in Italy in relation to certain business-to-government (B2G) transactions, where the VAT on supplies to public entities is retained by those entities and remitted directly to tax authorities. As discussed below, the United Kingdom has carried out a consultation on the introduction of split payment for certain supplies (which would require some form of VAT collection by the payment services providers).

In a similar way, Australia will require purchasers of newly constructed residential properties to remit GST directly to tax authorities as part of the settlement. Under the current law (where the GST is included in the purchase price and the developer remits the GST to tax authorities), some developers are failing to remit the GST despite having claimed GST credits on their construction costs. As most purchasers use legal services for the transfer of the property to complete their purchase, they are expected to experience minimal impact from the new measure. The measure will become effective on 1 July 2018.

The United Kingdom stepped up efforts to combat VAT fraud in online sales, building on an earlier package of measures. The new measure will hold online marketplaces "jointly and severally" liable for any future unpaid VAT by a domestic or foreign seller on their platforms.[23] Online marketplaces will be required to check the validity of sellers' VAT numbers and online sellers will have to display their VAT number on the online marketplace. The government is also considering the introduction of VAT split payments for online purchases.

Finally, international administrative cooperation and exchange of information are increasingly being considered to combat VAT fraud and evasion. Governments increasingly recognise that information exchange and administrative co-operation play a significant role in combatting international VAT fraud and ensuring effective tax collection in the context of the digitalisation of the economy. This need was emphasised in the 2018 OECD Report on *Tax Challenges Arising from Digitalisation* and scoping OECD work in this area is ongoing. In the EU, such cooperation is supported by 'Eurofisc', the EU's network of anti-fraud experts, and the European Commission has proposed reinforcing administrative cooperation in November 2017, with an online system for real-time information sharing and operational cooperation between Member States' tax administrations and law enforcement authorities. A bilateral exchange of information agreement was also signed between the EU and Norway in February 2018.

Progress on the taxation of inbound digital services has continued

Over 50 jurisdictions have already implemented the Guidelines for the treatment of cross-border supplies of services and intangibles. The OECD International VAT/GST Guidelines have been endorsed as the international standard to ensure a coherent and efficient application of VAT/GST to international trade in services (see Box 3.9). As discussed in the previous edition of this report, the elements of the Guidelines that have received most attention since 2016 were the recommended rules and mechanisms for the effective collection of VAT on B2C supplies of services and intangibles (including digital supplies) by foreign suppliers. The Guidelines recommend that the right to tax these supplies for VAT purposes be allocated to the country where the customer has its usual residence and that foreign suppliers of these services and intangibles register and remit VAT in the country of the customer's usual residence. The Guidelines also recommend the implementation of a simplified registration and compliance regime to facilitate compliance for foreign suppliers.

Box 3.10. OECD International VAT/GST Guidelines

At the OECD Global Forum on VAT in November 2015, more than 100 countries and jurisdictions endorsed the new OECD International VAT/GST Guidelines as the international standard to ensure a coherent and efficient application of VAT/GST to international trade in services. The Guidelines were incorporated into an OECD Recommendation by the OECD Council in September 2016.

In the absence of these Guidelines, there was no internationally agreed framework for the application of VAT to cross-border trade, in contrast with existing frameworks for the taxation of income such as the OECD Model Tax Convention and the Transfer Pricing Guidelines. This led to increasing uncertainty and complexity for both tax authorities and businesses and risks of double taxation and unintended non-taxation. This was a matter of special concern with respect to international trade in services and intangibles, which has considerably increased over the last decade. Thus, the Guidelines provide a framework to promote greater tax certainty, facilitation of trade and to increase tax revenues for countries.

The Guidelines include chapters on the principle of VAT neutrality and its implementation in practice, and on the implementation of the destination principle for allocating the taxing rights on cross-border supplies of services and intangibles. For business-to-business supplies the Guidelines establish that, the taxing rights on cross border supplies of services and intangibles are to be allocated to the jurisdiction where the business customer has located its permanent business presence. For business-to-consumer supplies, the Guidelines recommend that the taxing rights over "on-the-spot supplies" be allocated to the jurisdiction in which the supply is physically performed; and that the taxing rights over all other supplies and services be allocated to the jurisdiction in which the customer has its usual residence. These include remote supplies of services and digital products over the Internet (e.g. apps, streaming of music and movies, online gaming) by foreign suppliers. The Guidelines recommend that these foreign suppliers be required to register and remit VAT in the jurisdiction of taxation and that countries implement a simplified registration and compliance regime to facilitate compliance for non-resident suppliers. They finally recommend that the taxing rights be allocated to the jurisdiction where immovable property is located when they are closely connected with such property.

The Guidelines do not aim at providing detailed prescriptions for national legislation. Jurisdictions are sovereign with respect to the design and application of their laws. Rather, the Guidelines seek to identify objectives and suggest means for achieving them, thereby serving as a reference point. Global Forum participants urged the OECD and G20 to develop implementation packages to support the consistent implementation of the Guidelines and to design an even more inclusive framework that would involve all interested countries and jurisdictions, particularly developing countries, on an equal footing.

In respect of the desired development of implementation packages, the OECD published a report in 2017 on 'Mechanisms for the effective Collection of VAT/GST'. This report provides valuable practical guidance for countries who wish to tax inbound digital services in cases where the supplier is not located in the jurisdiction with the taxing rights.

Argentina, South Africa and Turkey are among the countries that have recently introduced changes to ensure or enhance the taxation of inbound digital services. In Argentina, digital services provided by foreign companies including the access to or downloading of videos, music, games and other services consumed in Argentina are now taxed at a VAT rate of 21%. In most cases, the system requires financial intermediaries to act as tax collecting and paying agents. South Africa also made amendments to the taxation of digital services. Non-resident suppliers of digital services have been required to register for and collect South African VAT since June 2014. The new amendments include removing a number of exemptions on e-services and requiring intermediaries and online platforms issuing invoices on such supplies to register. Turkey now also requires non-resident suppliers of digital services to register for and collect Turkish VAT on their sales to local customers.

New measures are being introduced to collect VAT on the imports of low-value goods

Most countries provide VAT relief regimes for low-value imports. These were mainly motivated by the consideration that the costs of collecting VAT on imported low-value items would likely outweigh the VAT actually collected. At the time when most of these relief regimes were introduced, online shopping did not exist and the level of imports benefitting from the relief was relatively small. However, there has been a significant and rapid growth in the volume of low value imports of physical goods on which VAT is not collected. This has resulted in large potential VAT revenues not being collected and growing risks of unfair competition for domestic retailers who are required to charge VAT on their sales to domestic consumers. It also creates an incentive for domestic suppliers to relocate to an offshore jurisdiction to sell their low-value goods free of VAT. The 2015 BEPS Action 1 Report concluded that governments could be in a position to remove or lower their exemption thresholds for imports of low-value goods and suggested different approaches to increase the efficiency of VAT collection on such imports (OECD, 2015[18]) (Box 3.10).

Australia is a first mover in this area, extending GST to imports of low-value goods. As of 1 July 2018, Australia will repeal its GST relief for imports of goods with value of AUD 1 000 or less supplied by foreign vendors to Australian final consumers.[24] The GST on those imports will be collected and remitted by the foreign vendors through a simplified registration-based collection regime where foreign vendors that supply more than AUD 75 000 of taxable goods to consumers in Australia per year, will be required to register for GST in Australia and charge the tax on their sales to final consumers in Australia. This threshold of AUD 75 000 (which is the same as the one below which local businesses are relieved from the collection of the GST) aims at avoiding the registration of small traders for which the cost of collection would be too high. If goods are purchased via an online marketplace, the online marketplace will be treated as the supplier of the goods and will therefore be responsible for collecting and remitting the GST.

Switzerland is also seeking to level the playing field between domestic and foreign companies by amending its VAT registration rules. As of 2018, the new rules to determine whether companies have to register for Swiss VAT are based on global turnover as opposed to Swiss turnover. Foreign suppliers of goods and (certain) services are liable to register for VAT in Switzerland and collect the tax on supplies to Swiss customers where their global taxable turnover exceeds CHF 100 000. The second major change concerns foreign (online) retailers selling low-value goods to Swiss customers. Currently, VAT on imports is only levied if the VAT amount exceeds CHF 5. The low

VAT rates of 2.5% and 7.7% (as of 1 January 2018) imply that goods up to a value of CHF 200 (taxable at 2.5%) and CHF 65 (taxable at 7.7%) can be imported VAT-free. To remove this competitive advantage for foreign suppliers, from 1 January 2019, businesses that send such small consignments to Switzerland for a total amount of at least CHF 100 000 will be required to register for and remit VAT in Switzerland.

EU countries have agreed on new rules to enhance and simplify VAT compliance for e-commerce in goods. Key measures include allowing businesses selling goods to their customers online to deal with their VAT obligations in the EU through a single online portal; the removal of the current VAT relief for imports from outside the EU of goods valued under EUR 22; and simplified rules for businesses with intra-EU cross-border sales of less than EUR 100 000. In addition, large online marketplaces will be responsible for ensuring that VAT is collected on sales that are made by non-EU companies to EU consumers via their platforms. These changes will become effective gradually by 2021 (European Commission, 2017[19]). The EU and the Australian reforms on digital platforms are feeding into current OECD work (see Box 3.10).

Box 3.11. Addressing the VAT/GST challenges arising from digitalisation

The fast development of new technologies has dramatically increased the ability of private consumers to engage in online shopping as well as the capability of businesses to directly reach customers globally without any physical presence in market jurisdictions, resulting in an inappropriately low amount of VAT being collected on supplies by foreign sellers and in an uneven playing field between domestic suppliers and foreign suppliers.

The 2015 BEPS Action 1 Report outlined how highly digitalised businesses could structure their affairs so that little or no VAT is paid on remotely delivered services and intangibles, and concluded that the OECD's International VAT/GST Guidelines provided the solution. In accordance with the destination principle, they allow tax authorities to collect VAT on inbound cross-border supplies of services and intangibles in the jurisdiction where the customer is located. The 2015 BEPS Action 1 Report also recommends that the foreign supplier be allowed to register for VAT in the market jurisdiction under a simplified registration and compliance regime for B2C supplies and outlines options to facilitate the collection of VAT on the importation of low-value goods from online sales.

Implementation

To date, over 50 jurisdictions, including a large majority of OECD and G20 countries, have adopted rules for the VAT treatment of B2C supplies of services and intangibles by foreign suppliers in accordance with the OECD International VAT/GST Guidelines. Further guidance was developed in 2017 to support governments in the implementation of best practices in the design and operation of the collection mechanism recommended by the 2015 BEPS Action 1 Report and the OECD International VAT/GST Guidelines, which has been included in the report on "*Mechanisms for the Effective Collection of VAT/GST Where the Supplier Is Not Located in the Jurisdiction of Taxation*" published on 24 October 2017. This work has already greatly enhanced compliance levels by promoting more consistent and effective implementation of the agreed approaches. Early data on the impact of these measures is very promising with revenue in excess of EUR 3 billion collected via the EU simplified compliance regime in 2015 alone. This allowed businesses to achieve a reduction in their compliance burden that is estimated to be 95% lower than it would have been without such simplification measures.

Future work on digital platforms

One of the broader tax challenges arising from digitalisation relates to the collection of VAT on cross-border trade in goods, services and intangibles, particularly where private consumers acquire them from suppliers abroad. Further work is being carried out by the OECD Working Party No.9 on Consumption Taxes (WP9) to promote the consistent implementation and operation of the recommended rules. This work is focusing on the role of online platforms and other intermediaries in the VAT collection process through an analysis of (i) the functions performed by digital platforms in online sales and delivery chains and (ii) the possible role of platforms performing these functions in the collection of VAT on online sales. A report with guidance and best practices is scheduled to be completed before the end of 2018.

Excise duty rates have continued to increase, especially for tobacco ***products***

Excise taxes, which are only levied on specific goods, have increasingly been used to influence consumer behaviour. Excise taxes on tobacco and alcohol have traditionally been introduced for revenue-raising purposes. More recently, however, they have also been used as corrective taxation tools, to discourage the consumption of products that generate negative externalities or internalities. In the case of tobacco, for instance, the relatively low price elasticity of demand for tobacco products, the small number of producers and significant consumption initially made tobacco products particularly attractive targets for excise taxation to raise revenue. In recent decades, with mounting evidence of the health consequences of tobacco use and on the effectiveness of increased tobacco taxation in reducing consumption (World Health Organization, 2015[20]), tobacco taxation has also become a key tool to improve public health.

Last year, a large number of countries reported excise duty increases. Excise duty increases on tobacco products were particularly numerous. A more limited number of countries raised excise duties on alcoholic beverages. Reported reforms also confirmed the increasing popularity of taxes on soft drinks, with several countries either introducing or considering the introduction of such taxes.

Increases in excise duties, especially on tobacco products, have continued this year. A number of countries have raised their excise taxes on alcoholic beverages and tobacco products with the double objective of raising revenues and improving health outcomes (Table 3.11). As in previous years, increases in excise duties have been more popular for tobacco than alcohol. Excise tax increases on tobacco products were introduced in 13 countries in 2017 and in seven countries in 2018. Regarding alcoholic beverages, excise tax increases were introduced in four countries in both 2017 and 2018. On the other hand, the United Kingdom froze alcohol duties for 2018.

Table 3.11. Excise tax increases on alcohol and tobacco products

	Rate/Base ⇧	
Into effect in	2017	2018 or later
Alcoholic beverages	EST ISL PRT SWE	ARG EST FIN ZAF
Tobacco products	AUS EST GBR GRC HUN IRL ISL LUX LVA NZL PRT SVK SVN	ARG[1] BEL CAN FIN FRA NLD ZAF

Note: [1] Decrease in the *ad valorem* tax rate from 75% to 70% but increase in the minimum tax per pack.
Source: OECD Annual Tax Policy Reform Questionnaire.

New excise taxes on other types of harmful consumption are being introduced

New excise duties are being introduced on other types of consumption. Countries are increasingly seeking to extend specific taxes on the consumption of products that generate negative externalities and internalities beyond traditional tobacco and alcohol taxes. In some cases, new excise taxes are also being introduced to harmonise the tax treatment between close substitutes.

New or higher taxes are being levied on alternatives to cigarettes. Sweden and Poland introduced new taxes on e-cigarettes, following Greece and Finland which reported the introduction of new e-cigarette taxes last year. In Poland, the new excise tax will be levied on two new categories of goods: novel tobacco products and liquids used in electronic cigarettes. In addition to raising additional revenue, the measure aims to ensure a more equal tax treatment between traditional tobacco products, electronic cigarettes and new tobacco products. In Korea, the tax on heat-not-burn tobacco products, which as opposed to e-cigarettes actually contain tobacco but do not produce smoke, was raised.

In Canada, a framework for cannabis taxation was established. A federal excise duty framework for cannabis products will come into effect when cannabis for non-medical purposes becomes accessible for retail sale in 2018. Excise duties will be imposed on federally licensed producers at the higher of a flat rate applied on the quantity of cannabis contained in the final product or a percentage of the sale price of the product sold by a federal licensee. Cannabis products containing low amounts of Tetrahydrocannabinol will generally not be subject to the excise duty, and pharmaceutical products derived from cannabis will also be exempt, provided that the cannabis product has a Drug Identification Number and can only be acquired through a prescription.

Three new taxes on sugar-sweetened beverages, announced last year, are coming into effect this year. Ireland, the United Kingdom and South Africa are introducing a tax on sugar-sweetened drinks in 2018. The taxes in the United Kingdom and Ireland are very similar, with a first rate applying to drinks with a total sugar content between 5g and 8g per 100 ml, and a higher rate for drinks with 8g or more per 100 ml. In South Africa, the "health promotion levy" is imposed on soft drinks with a sugar content exceeding 4g per 100 ml. Existing health-related taxes in Belgium (on sugar-sweetened beverages) and in Norway (on chocolate and sugar and non-alcoholic beverages) have also been raised; and Turkey extended its special consumption tax to fruit juices and all sodas (previously the tax was only imposed on cola).

Finally, South Africa has reported using excise taxes to enhance fairness. *Ad valorem* excise duty rates on luxury products (such as cosmetics and electronics) will be raised. Smart phones will be included in the revised classification of mobile phones to ensure that they attract *ad valorem* excise duties and the government will consult on a proposal to replace the flat rate with progressive rates based on the value of phones. Finally, the maximum *ad valorem* excise duty for motor vehicles will be raised from 25% to 30%. These measures are not expected to bring in significant revenue but aim to enhance fairness by increasing taxes on products consumed mainly by wealthier households.

Environmentally-related taxes

Overall, this section shows that environmentally-related tax reforms have continued to focus on energy taxes but that efforts have been made to go beyond road transport. While these changes go in the right direction, they have occurred only in a few countries and more significant reforms will be needed to align energy tax rates with environmental costs and generate additional tax revenues. Changes to vehicle taxes to encourage the use of cleaner vehicles have continued, but experience has shown that – while effective – they can be a costly emissions reduction policy. Finally, despite their large potential to generate environmental improvements, tax reforms outside of energy and vehicles, such as taxes on waste, plastic bags or chemicals, have been much less frequent.

In general, environmentally-related taxes remain widely underused

Governments face mounting environmental challenges, including climate change, threats to biodiversity, air pollution and waste management. Tax policy can help address these challenges. By increasing the relative prices of environmentally harmful goods, taxes can directly address the market failure that causes markets to ignore environmental costs, and ensure that consumers take these costs into account in spending decisions. Taxes are not only an effective tool to reduce pollution and other environmentally harmful behaviours but, by shifting the decision of how to best adapt behaviour towards consumers, taxes also minimise the costs at which these reductions are achieved. More broadly, aligning tax policy with environmental policy goals allows attaining environmental objectives more smoothly and rapidly.

Environmentally-related taxes are any compulsory, unrequited payment to general government on tax bases deemed of particular environmental relevance. Tax bases include – but are not limited to – energy, transport, waste and chemicals. The underlying policy intent for using these taxes can vary and differs strongly across the different environmentally-related tax bases. For instance, while energy taxes are usually levied with revenue-raising objectives in mind, taxes on waste or chemicals tend to be introduced to steer consumers towards more environmentally friendly behaviours (OECD, 2017[21]).

Despite their proven appeal as growth-friendly fiscal and environmental policy instruments, environmentally-related taxes remain widely underused. Across almost all environmental policy domains, tax rates are set below the social costs of harmful behaviours and tax bases remain narrow. This constrains the potential of environmentally-related taxes to raise revenue and trigger behavioural adjustments. In addition, tax rate and base increases continue to unfold very gradually, suggesting that there is still ample room for using environmentally-related taxes to achieve environmental and tax policy objectives (OECD, 2018[22]; OECD, 2017[23]).

The interactions between fiscal and environmental policy objectives are not limited to environmentally-related taxes. For example, tax incentives are often used to promote private R&D, and can be targeted at low-carbon technologies. Current market conditions and path dependence – both geared towards high-carbon technologies – as well as the large knowledge spillovers from patents in low-carbon technologies can justify using these tax incentives under certain circumstances (Dechezleprêtre, Martin and Mohnen, 2013[24]; Dechezleprêtre, Martin and Bassi, 2016[25]). Misalignments between tax and environmental policy objectives can also arise in CIT, where provisions to recover capital costs are not entirely technology-neutral. For example, Dressler et al. (2018[26]) show that CIT rules for cost recovery sometimes imply higher effective tax rates for technologies characterised by high capital costs relative to their counterparts which rely more intensively on variable costs (e.g. fuel costs) when investment is equity-financed. Because renewable electricity is relatively capital-intensive, this can result in an unintentional misalignment of the CIT system with policy objectives relating to decarbonisation (Dressler, Hanappi and van Dender, 2018[26]) (Box 3.11).

Box 3.12. The potential for tax induced technology-bias against renewable electricity

Fiscal policies that explicitly intend to help preserve the climate, such as carbon pricing, are implemented in the presence of existing policies and regulation. Misalignments between climate goals and the existing policy framework can and do exist, but are sometimes not straightforward to identify. For example, corporate income tax (CIT) provisions for cost recovery may in some cases inadvertently weaken incentives to invest in power plants relying on renewable energy sources rather than in power plants based on fossil fuels.

This unintentional technology-bias of CIT is driven by differences in cost structure across power plant technologies. Typically electricity generation technologies based on renewable sources of energy, such as solar, feature relatively high capital costs and low variable costs per unit of output, as they do not incur substantial fuel costs. In contrast, technologies relying on fossil-fuels (e.g. gas), are characterised by relatively high variable costs, as they include the market price of fuel.

Evaluating CIT provisions for cost recovery across 36 OECD and partner economies, in particular the immediate deductibility of variable costs and country-specific rules to depreciate capital costs, shows that a technology-bias from differences in cost structures may exist and that the extent and existence of this bias depends on the financing structure of a power plant investment: When the investment is debt-financed, tax systems can treat capital costs in a way that produces technology-neutral results. In contrast, current CIT rules are not technology neutral across equity-financed investments, even if fiscal depreciation rules follow an asset's useful life. When an investment is equity-financed, the capital cost deduction may effectively be seen to be inadequate in the typical circumstance where the cost of equity is not deductible.

As a consequence, average effective tax rates are relatively higher for capital-cost-intensive electricity generation when investment is financed by equity. Since electricity generation based on renewables tends to be relatively capital-intensive, this result can be seen as a form of unintentional misalignment of the CIT system with decarbonisation objectives.

In countries where renewable investments use relatively more debt than equity finance to cover capital costs, this bias against renewables is somewhat muted. However, given the limited data available, no strong conclusion about financing patterns can be made at this stage.

Source: (Dressler, Hanappi and van Dender, 2018$_{[26]}$)

Environmentally-related tax revenues continue to be driven by energy taxes

Revenues from environmentally-related taxes in 2014 varied widely across countries, from 0.06% of GDP in Mexico[25] to 4.1% of GDP in Denmark (Figure 3.16). High revenue shares from environmentally-related taxes can result from high tax rates but also from high levels of pollution. Looking at trends over time, environmentally-related tax revenues have tended to fall since the mid-1990s. Between 1995 and 2014, environmentally-related tax revenue as a share of GDP fell in the majority of the countries covered in the report, and remained stable in some. A combination of factors, including declining real tax rates, fuel use reductions resulting from higher energy taxes and prices, oil price increases, and the effects of other overlapping environmental policies, could explain these declining shares of environmentally-related tax revenue in GDP (OECD, 2017[23]). Environmentally-related tax revenues as a share of GDP increased in eight countries, though the policy contexts behind these increases differ widely. On average, across all countries, environmentally-related taxes raised 2.2% of GDP in 2014, a share roughly similar to their levels in 2005 (2.2%) and 1995 (2.2%).

In line with past trends, more than half of environmentally-related tax revenues are raised through energy taxes. Motor vehicle taxes and other taxes on transport are the second largest component of environmentally-related tax revenues. Given the policy changes in environmentally-related taxes for 2018 discussed below and those observed in previous years, energy taxes are likely to remain by far the largest source of environmentally-related tax revenues.

Figure 3.16. Revenues from environmentally-related taxes as a share of GDP by country in 1995, 2005 and 2014

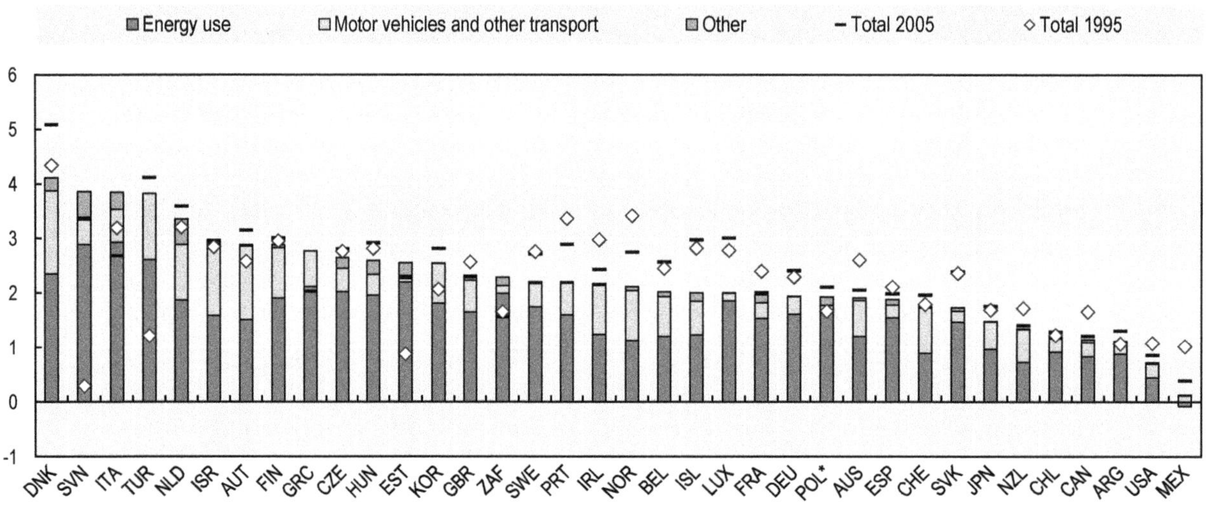

Source: OECD Database on Policy Instruments for the Environment.

In recent years, road fuel taxes have become even more predominant, while the scope for raising tax rates outside of road transport remains large

Road fuel taxes contribute significantly to environmentally-related tax revenues, and tax rates exceed those on other fuels and sectors by far (Panel A of Figure 3.17). In 2015, in the 42 OECD and G20 countries for which comparable data is collected by the OECD and which together account for 80% of carbon emissions from energy use, nearly all carbon emissions from energy use in road transport were subject to a tax. Effective tax rates exceed a low-end estimate of the climate costs of carbon emissions of EUR 30 per tCO_2 for 50% of emissions (OECD, 2018[22]). These findings do not imply that tax rates on road fuels are high enough or excessive, however, because this estimate of EUR 30 per tCO_2 only considers climate costs and does not take into account the other negative side effects of fuel use in road transport. These additional negative direct and indirect side effects (e.g. congestion and air pollution) are large, indicating that tax rates on road fuels may be approaching the right level in a few high-tax countries, but remain well below these costs in most others (Van Dender, 2018[27]).

Between 2012 and 2015, the predominance of road fuel taxes increased even further. Increases in the effective tax rates in road transport were primarily driven by fuel tax reforms in China, India and Mexico. Decreases have occurred too, both due to shifts to lower taxed fuels and inflation eroding real tax rates in some high-tax countries (OECD, 2018[22]).

Tax rates are much lower outside of road transport and reform efforts have been slow. Outside of road transport, 81% of emissions are untaxed, and rates are above the low-end estimate of climate costs for just 3% of emissions (Panel B of Figure 3.17). This is very concerning since 85% of carbon emissions from energy use in 42 OECD and G20 economies occur outside of road transport. Changes in tax rates between 2012 and 2015 were modest, though some encouraging country-level initiatives can be identified (OECD, 2018[22]). For example, India and Korea introduced broad-based taxes on coal use, and both countries have since then increased the rates of these taxes.

Figure 3.17. Proportion of carbon emissions from energy use subject to different levels of effective tax rates in the road and non-road sectors, in 2012 and 2015

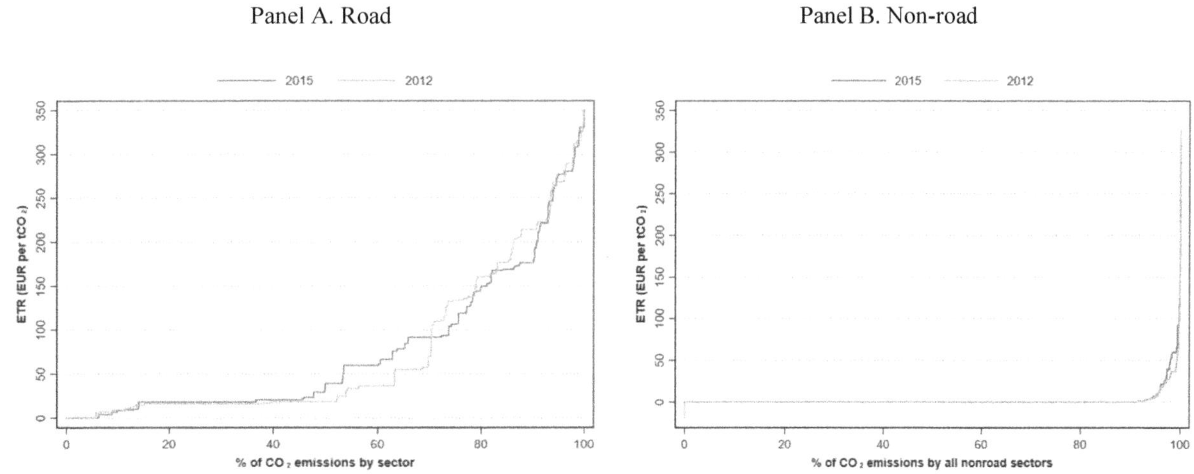

Note: All tax rates are expressed in 2012 prices. Carbon emissions from biomass emissions are included.
Source: OECD (2018d).

Despite these changes, the energy tax landscape remains widely misaligned with key principles of environmental taxation. Better aligning taxes with environmental costs would suggest increasing almost all taxes (including on road fuels, see above), while achieving carbon abatement at lowest cost would require increased uniformity of taxes across different sectors and fuels. However, in 2015, tax rates continued to differ widely across sectors and fuels (Figure 3.18). Tax rates are particularly low in the different non-road sectors, and they differ widely by fuel. Coal, characterised by high levels of harmful emissions, is taxed at the lowest rates by far, while oil products are taxed at the highest effective rates. If countries want to increase the alignment of tax rates with carbon and other external costs, and increase tax revenues at the same time, gradual increases in tax rates on lower taxed sectors and fuels are warranted.

Figure 3.18. Effective tax rates on carbon emissions from energy use, 2015 (including carbon emissions from biomass, excluding taxes on electricity output)

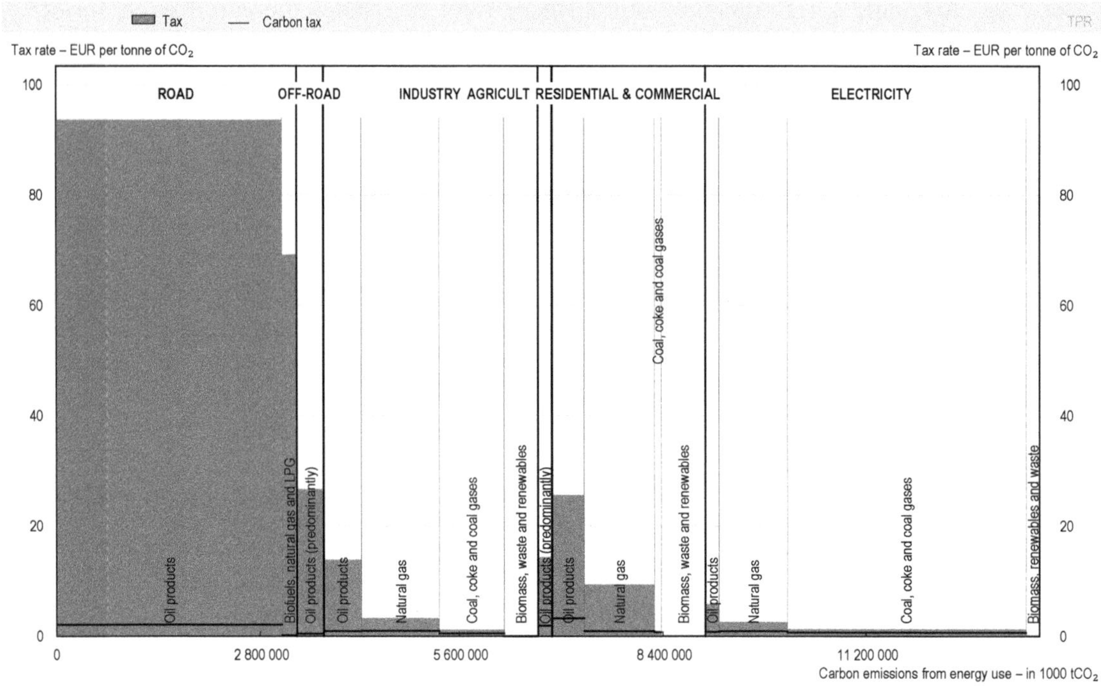

Source: Adapted based on OECD (2018d).

Permit prices in CO_2 emissions trading systems change energy prices in ways that are similar to carbon taxes or other specific taxes on energy use. Though permit prices in many emission trading schemes (ETS) tend to be low, they apply fairly broadly in the industry and electricity sectors and strengthen carbon prices considerably in some countries (OECD, 2016[28]). Some countries made progress in carbon pricing by implementing ETSs in recent years. China launched a nation-wide system at the end of 2017, and Canada is giving provinces the choice to follow a pre-determined carbon price path through the implementation of either carbon taxes or trading systems. Permit prices are not included in Figure 3.17 and Figure 3.18, but are covered in the OECD's *Effective Carbon Rates* (OECD, 2016[28]).

In line with past trends, environmentally-related tax reforms have largely revolved around energy taxes in 2018

Among the environmentally-related tax reforms implemented in 2018, energy tax increases have been the most frequent and the most significant in terms of their expected revenue effects (Table 3.12). Six countries increased taxes on specific fuels across all sectors, and three countries (France, Iceland and Norway) increased their specific taxes on carbon. Belgium, France, Sweden and South Africa implemented tax increases targeted at transport fuels. In line with past trends, the stated objective of most of these energy tax increases has been to improve environmental sustainability, but revenue-raising considerations were important too. The new Dutch government has also announced a range of significant energy and other environmental tax proposals to enhance environmental sustainability which could enter into force in 2019 and 2020 (Box 3.12).

Energy tax decreases occurred in three countries. As discussed below, Sweden reformed road fuel taxes to adjust to a new blending requirement for biofuels. Mexico is extending a price smoothing mechanism for road transport fuels. The United Kingdom reported a freeze in fuel tax rates, translating into real rate decreases over time, but energy tax rates have remained nominally unchanged in many other countries too.

Table 3.12. Changes to taxes on energy use

	Rate/Base ⇧		**Rate/Base ⇩**	
Into effect in	**2017**	**2018 or later**	**2017**	**2018 or later**
Fuels, with sector specification:				
Electricity production	KOR LVA (GBR[c])	(NLD)	GRC	
Agriculture		ESP		
Heating and process	FIN FIN[c]	FIN	GRC	
Transport	BEL EST FIN GRC ISL ISL[c] MEX PRT NOR[c] (EST)	BEL, FRA, SWE[b], ZAF		SWE, MEX
Specific fuels, all sectors	EST (EST)	BEL[i], FRA, KOR, LVA, NLD, (NLD), SWE[i]	GBR	GBR[i]
Carbon tax	CAN[1] (GBR)	ISL, FRA, NOR (NLD), (ZAF)		
Electricity consumption	SWE		DNK SWE[2]	DNK, (NLD)

Note: Countries in brackets have only announced reforms.
[1] carbon tax in Alberta.
[2] revenue is expected to increase through economic growth effects.
[b] tax related to biofuels.
[c] tax based on the carbon content of fuels.
[i] taxes were indexed to inflation.
Source: OECD Annual Tax Policy Reform Questionnaire.

Box 3.13. The environmental tax proposals in the Dutch Coalition Agreement

The Coalition Agreement of the new Dutch government (2017 to 2021) includes a number of environmental tax policy changes to be implemented over the coming years. As part of a broader effort to accelerate domestic emissions reductions and push for greater climate ambition at European (EU) level, it is proposed to introduce a national minimum price under the EU ETS. This would mean introducing a national tax on electricity generation fuels and charging companies for the difference between the tax and permit prices. The tax would start at EUR 18 per tCO_2 in 2020, rising to EUR 43 per tCO_2 by 2030.The Dutch proposal for a price floor is contingent on efforts to strengthen carbon trading at the EU level. The Dutch proposal has been made against the background of some countries that consider the EU ETS permit prices are too low to reach climate goals proposing a system-wide minimum price (Reuters, 2018[29]). At the same time, other countries have taken unilateral action. As an example, the price floor introduced by the United Kingdom in 2013 (currently applying at GBP 18 per tCO_2) is estimated to have driven the significant decreases in electricity generated from coal domestically (Hirst, 2018[30]). As the ETS-wide amount of emissions permits remained unchanged, permits unused in the United Kingdom could be used elsewhere in the trading system (a phenomenon termed the 'waterbed effect'). The waterbed effect will decline with the start of the market stability reserve in 2019 and the cancellation of allowances in the reserve as of 2023, which are part of the revision of the EU ETS directive.

To reach the newly set stricter climate targets mentioned above, the Netherlands will also phase out electricity generation from coal before 2030. Other environmental tax measures announced include a reduction in the tax-free threshold for energy consumption, a tax shift away from electricity towards natural gas to better reflect the carbon content of fuels, and a new tax on waste. In the absence of sufficient emissions reductions in aviation, a new tax on air tickets will be introduced in 2021, though preference is given to introducing an EU-wide tax on air tickets. Together, these proposals are expected to translate into significant revenue increases.

Some countries have implemented measures to align tax rates more closely with the carbon content of fuels

A number of countries have implemented tax reforms to increase the uniformity of the tax treatment of different fuels outside of road transport, taking steps towards a better reflection of the polluter-pays-principle in energy taxation. To achieve this, Iceland, France and Norway have increased their specific taxes on carbon in all sectors, while in Finland the energy and carbon tax increases are limited to heating fuels. Following a broad consultation with industry and other stakeholders since the publication of a first discussion paper in 2010, South Africa proposed the introduction of a carbon tax from 2019. The stated purpose of the carbon tax is to achieve the country's commitment to emissions reductions under the Paris Agreement. The proposed basic rate is ZAR 120 (around EUR 8[26]) and the tax will be accompanied by a range of tax incentives, tax credits and tax-shifting measures to minimise its impact on electricity prices and energy-intensive sectors. As mentioned above, carbon prices – including energy taxes, carbon taxes and emissions trading systems – can be cost-effective instruments to achieve emissions reductions. However, experience has shown that carbon tax bases are often narrow, and their tax rates usually lie below a minimum estimate of climate costs, which can limit their effectiveness (OECD, 2018[22]).

Increasing specific taxes on low-taxed fuels is another way to align environmental costs more closely with fuel prices. In 2018, Korea further increased its tax on coal, traditionally taxed at low rates, and France is increasing its specific tax on natural gas. However, given the scale of unpriced emissions, much stronger and broader moves are needed to achieve cost-effective emissions mitigation through emissions trading and taxes, and reach climate goals.

Compared to previous years, energy tax reforms have less frequently been targeted at road fuels, and the types of policy changes affecting road fuel taxes have been diverse. In a welcome move, two road fuel taxes in South Africa were increased – from a relatively low level – to compensate for inflation. In an effort to decrease the carbon intensity of road transport fuels, Sweden introduced a new blending requirement of fossil fuels with biofuels. To offset expected price increases from this requirement, Sweden lowered the energy tax on road fuels and extended the carbon tax to biofuels used in road transport. Mexico – which has recently implemented a large environmental tax and subsidy reform, resulting in road fuel prices being more closely aligned with market conditions (Arlinghaus and van Dender, 2017[31]) – reacted to the recent rise in oil prices by extending the price smoothing mechanism applied to gasoline and diesel. This "fiscal stimulus" applies in addition to the excise tax on road fuels and buffers international oil price fluctuations on the domestic market. Since oil prices are currently on the rise, the stimulus is expected to reduce tax levels and revenues.

Belgium and France are continuing to gradually align the taxation of gasoline and diesel with the external costs of each fuel, but in general countries' efforts to narrow the differential taxation between diesel and gasoline decreased compared to 2017. At the current state of equipment and technology, diesel usually emits higher levels of harmful air pollutants per litre than gasoline and its carbon content is higher. On externality grounds, this suggests that diesel should be taxed at higher rates than gasoline, but diesel remains taxed at lower effective tax rates than gasoline in all but two of the countries covered in this report (Figure 3.19).

In 2018, two countries have moved towards automatically linking tax rates to inflation. In the absence of indexation, inflation gradually erodes real tax rates and this has led to decreasing fuel tax revenues in many OECD and G20 countries (see above). In the case of Germany, Mahler et al. (2017[32]) estimate the revenues foregone from not indexing fuel tax rates in 2014 at EUR 5.6 billion (not accounting for behavioural adjustments). To address this issue, Belgium introduced the automatic indexation of energy taxes and Sweden is moving towards indexing all environmental taxes to inflation. The Swedish tax on natural gas and the waste tax will even be indexed to the Consumer Price Index (CPI) +2%, thus automatically strengthening tax levels and revenues over time. Moving in the opposite direction, the United Kingdom has extended the freeze in fuel tax rates to 2019, but tax rates have remained nominally unchanged in many other countries too.

Figure 3.19. Effective tax rates on gasoline and diesel for road use, 2015

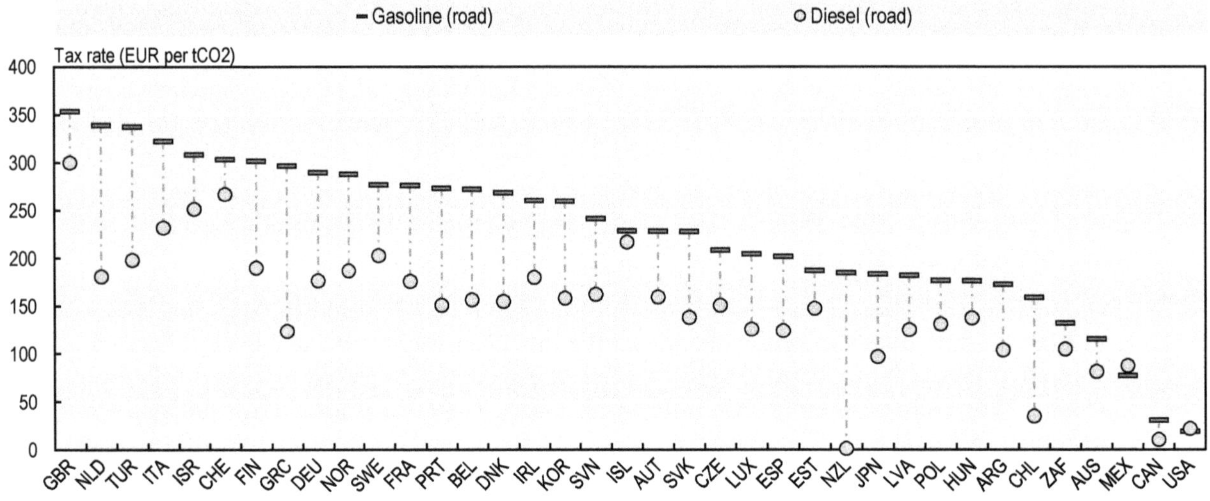

Source: Adapted based on OECD (2018d).

Within the transport sector, reforms have also focused on vehicle taxes and air travel

Overall, environmentally-related tax reforms in the transport sector have continued in 2018 with an emphasis on recurrent taxes on vehicles and registration taxes (Table 3.13). As in past years, many of these reforms have been targeted at increasing tax support for cars running on cleaner fuels (see below). Two countries (Argentina and Denmark) have implemented tax decreases for conventional cars.[27] Sweden introduced a new tax on air travel in 2018, and the Netherlands announced a new tax on air travel for 2021 if emissions reductions in air travel are insufficient and with a preference for introducing such a tax at the EU level (Vos, 2017[33]). Though many of these reforms indicate efforts to reduce pollution in the transport sector, as a whole they do not seem to reflect broad moves to align taxes more closely with the external costs of road and other transport modes.

Table 3.13. Changes to taxes on motor vehicles and other transport taxes

	Rate/Base ⇧		Rate/Base ⇩	
Into effect in	2017	2018 or later	2017	2018 or later
Vehicle tax	LVA[1] PRT	GBR ZAF	LVA[1] NOR[2]	ARG
Registration tax	(EST GBR)	(NLD)	DNK NLD[1]	
Vehicles running on alternative fuels		NOR	DNK LUX SWE	IRL LUX SWE
Company cars	LUX		NLD[1]	
Air travel		SWE (NLD)		GBR
Other (e.g. luxury cars, scrappage schemes, purchase support)	LVA		AUS	

Note: Countries in brackets have only announced reforms.
[1] no impact in total revenue expected.
[2] part of a tax shift towards carbon content in automotive fuels.
Source: OECD Annual Tax Policy Reform Questionnaire.

Recurrent vehicle and registration taxes continue to be used to support the purchase of vehicles running on alternative fuels. In 2018, three countries (Ireland, Luxembourg and Sweden) increased tax support for hydrogen, electric or fuel cell cars. For example, in Sweden, a new bonus malus system was introduced, under which low-emission vehicles benefit from a bonus at purchase, while new highly polluting vehicles are taxed at higher rates for the first three years. In the United Kingdom, the vehicle tax reform targets air pollution from diesel cars, which has been shown to differ between laboratory and real-world driving conditions. Unless certified to meet Euro-6 emissions standards under real-world driving conditions, newly registered diesel cars in the United Kingdom are taxed at higher rates from 2018.

Using vehicle taxes to address air pollution can be effective to steer consumers towards purchasing cleaner cars, but tax design matters strongly for success. For example, classification by different rate bands can lead to the bunching of vehicle demand just below tax thresholds, and take away incentives to reduce emissions within the bands. In addition, vehicle taxes have been shown to be a relatively expensive way to reduce emissions and can result in high foregone tax revenues (Van Dender, 2018[26], and the sources cited therein). In Norway, large tax breaks contributed to strongly increasing the share of electric and hybrid vehicles in circulation (The Guardian, 2017[34]). However, in order to limit foregone revenue, the vehicle weight-based subsidy for hybrids was removed (Government of Norway, 2017[35]). Since heavy vehicles cause road wear and tear independent of the fuel they use, this is a welcome move, both from an externality pricing and a public finance perspective.

While some countries have reformed vehicle taxes, this does not seem to reflect broader moves towards a more consistent pricing of the different externalities from road transport. A practical policy mix to reduce air pollution in road transport consists of a mix of fuel taxes, distance charges – varying by time and place of driving and ideally also by vehicle type – and vehicle taxes (Van Dender, 2018[27]), but such broader tax and price changes have not been reported in 2018. In addition, other misalignments between tax and environmental policy, such as the frequent generous treatment of company cars and commuting costs under the personal income tax (Harding, 2014[36]; Roy, 2014[37]), or the under-pricing of parking, remain unaddressed in the environmentally-related tax reforms reported by countries for 2018.

Despite their large potential to generate environmental improvements, other environmentally-related tax reforms have been less frequent

In line with past years, tax reforms outside of transport and energy have been much less frequent (Table 3.14). From an environmental policy perspective, taxes on waste, plastic bags or chemicals can lead to strong adjustments in producer and consumer behaviour, and such taxes can be part of policy packages to move countries closer to the marginal-social-cost pricing of environmental externalities (Hogg et al., 2016[38]; OECD, 2017[23]). Hogg et al. (2016[38]) estimate that such a tax shift, which would involve greater uniformity in carbon and energy taxes, increased vehicle and aviation taxes, but also taxes on packaging, plastic bags, air and water pollution, pesticides, and fertilizers, would increase environmental tax revenues across the EU-28 from 2.6% to 3.6% of GDP.

In 2017, the Netherlands announced an increase in its tax on landfilling and incineration, followed by a broadening of the tax base to waste burned in bio-energy plants and the elimination of the exemption for sewage sludge. Taxes on landfill, typically levied on the weight or volume of waste delivered to landfill are in place in a number of European countries, and they have been shown to be successful in leading to better modes of depositing waste, i.e. towards recycling and composting (Watkins, 2012[39]). Incineration taxes are less common, but can also contribute to shifting waste towards better treatment modes (ibid.).

South Africa increased its tax on plastic bags by 50%, effective from April 2018. Taxes on plastic bags have been shown to be a very effective way to reduce their use and therefore to decrease plastic waste. For example, in the United Kingdom, following the introduction of a tax on plastic bags in 2015, the seven main retailers issued around 83% fewer bags (i.e. a reduction of over 6 billion bags) between April 2016 and April 2017, compared to 2014 (United Kingdom Department for Environment, 2017[40]). This is equivalent to each person in the population using 25 bags post-tax compared to 140 bags before the tax was introduced (ibid.). Recently, the British government indicated its intention to extend the GBP 0.05 charge per bag to shops with fewer than 250 employees (BBC, 2018[41]). Ireland is another example where the reductions in plastic bag litter, which accounted for 5% of litter pollution in 2001 compared to 0.13% in 2015, have been attributed to the Irish environmental levy on plastic bags (Institute for European Environmental Policy (IEEP), 2017[42]).

Table 3.14. Changes to other environmentally-related taxes

	Rate/Base ⇧		Rate/Base ⇩	
Into effect in	2017	2018 or later	2017	2018 or later
Chemicals	SWE			
Natural resources	LVA			
Waste		(NLD)		
Other	ZAF	ZAF		

Note: Countries in brackets have only announced reforms.
Source: OECD Annual Tax Policy Reform Questionnaire.

Property taxes

Overall, this section shows that 2018 has seen the introduction of a few significant property tax reforms. Compared to previous years, characterised by limited reforms both in number and in scope, a few notable property tax reforms have been introduced in 2018, including the doubling of the exemption threshold for the estate and gift tax in the United States, the introduction of a tax on securities accounts in Belgium, as well as France's repeal of the housing tax for 80% of households and the elimination of its net wealth tax which was replaced by a tax on real estate wealth.

Property taxes are generally a small source of revenue

Countries impose a variety of taxes on property. The most prominent property taxes across the countries covered in the report are recurrent taxes on immovable property, which are typically a key source of revenue for local governments. Property transaction taxes and inheritance and gift taxes are also common (Figure 3.20). A very small number of countries impose a tax on some measure of net wealth (Box 3.14).

Property tax revenues remain low in most countries. In 2016, the amount of revenues collected from property taxes varied quite widely across countries, ranging from 0.3% of GDP in Estonia to 4.3% of GDP in the United Kingdom. However, in a majority of countries, property taxes remain a small source of revenue. Trends in revenues in the last fifteen years have also differed across countries. Between 2000 and 2016, 20 countries reported increases in property tax revenues as a share of GDP while 16 recorded revenue falls. The largest revenue increases in percentage points were recorded by Argentina, Belgium, France, South Africa and Greece. On the other hand, Iceland, Sweden, Switzerland and Israel experienced the most significant property tax revenue falls in percentage points.

Figure 3.20. Property tax revenues as a share of GDP in 2000 and 2016, broken down by category

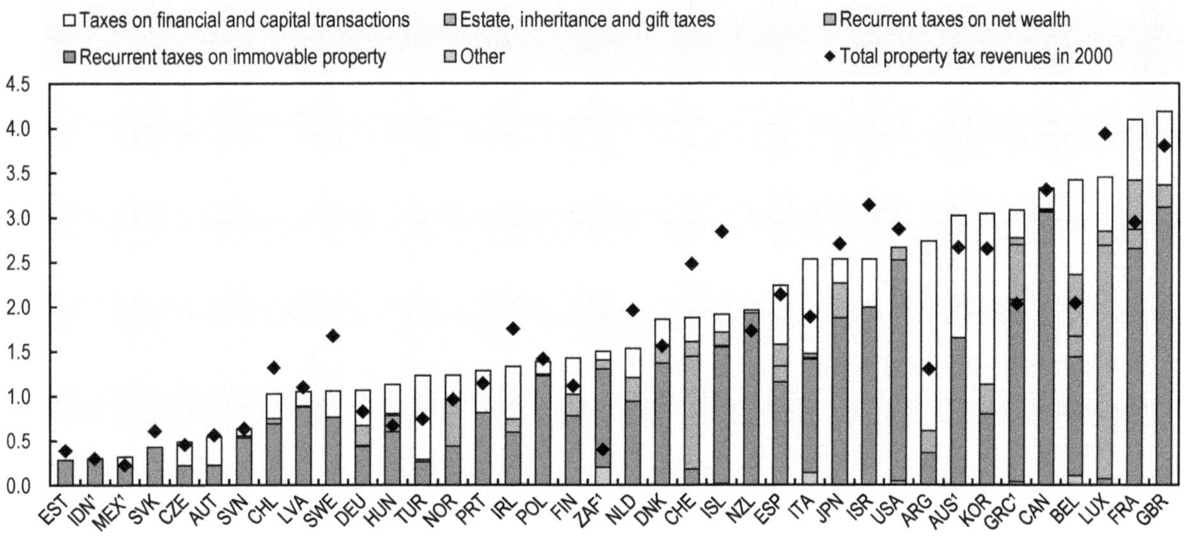

Note: [1] 2015 data used for Australia, Greece, Indonesia, Mexico and South Africa
Source: OECD and Global Revenue Statistics databases.

Longer-term trends show that property taxes are a smaller source of revenues than they used to be in the mid-1960s. Property tax revenues accounted for around 8% of total tax revenues on average in 1965 across OECD countries, compared to only about 6% today (Figure 3.21). The decline was particularly steep between 1965 and 1980, due to both diminishing property tax revenues as a share of GDP and an increase in overall tax revenues. Since the 1980s, property tax revenues have on average remained fairly stable.

Figure 3.21. Evolution of property tax revenues as a share of total taxation in the OECD since 1965

Property tax revenues as a share of total tax revenues – OECD unweighted average

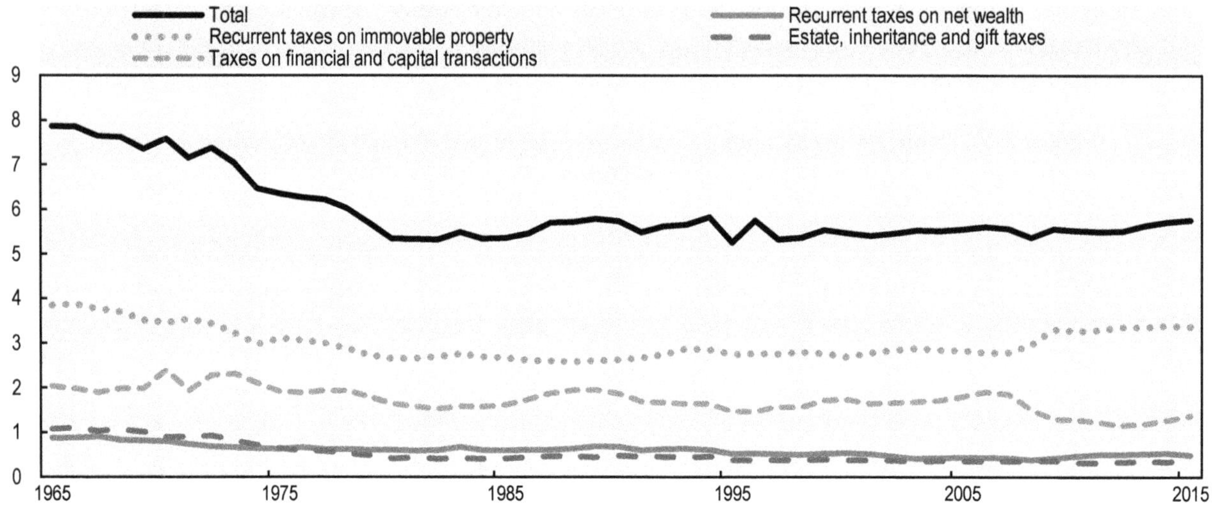

Source: OECD Revenue Statistics database.

A few significant property tax reforms were introduced in 2018

Compared to last year, 2018 has seen the introduction of more significant property tax reforms. Reforms introduced in 2017 were for the majority aimed at raising tax revenues (Table 3.15). The taxes that were raised generally included recurrent taxes on immovable property as well as transaction taxes on both movable and immovable property. Some reforms related to real estate taxation sought to "cool" housing markets by targeting investment in housing. Inheritance tax reforms, on the other hand, mostly involved tax reductions. However, these property tax reforms were generally limited in scope. By contrast, in 2018, a few countries introduced significant property tax reforms which are discussed below.

Table 3.15. Property tax changes

	Rate/Base⇧		Rate/Base⇩	
Into effect in	**2017**	**2018 or later**	**2017**	**2018 or later**
Estate duties, inheritance and gift taxes	DEU ZAF	TUR ZAF	DNK FIN GBR NLD[1]	USA
Transaction taxes on movable and immovable property	BEL FRA	BEL IRL		ARG GBR
Recurrent taxes on immovable property	FIN ISR PRT	FRA		FRA
Recurrent taxes on (net) wealth	LUX	BEL[2]	NOR	FRA NOR

Note:

[1] In the Netherlands, there was a temporary extension of the gift tax exemption in 2013-2014 and a structural extension from 2017.

[2] New tax on securities accounts in Belgium.

Source: OECD Annual Tax Policy Reform Questionnaire.

In the area of housing taxation, one of the most notable reforms was France's progressive repeal of the dwelling tax for 80% households. The dwelling tax (*taxe d'habitation*) is due annually by the household who occupies a dwelling (whether as owner or tenant). The repeal is being phased in over three years, with the tax reduction amounting to 30% in 2018, 65% in 2019 and 100% in 2020 for eligible households (i.e. below defined annual income thresholds). The dwelling tax has largely been perceived as unfair because the level of the tax varies widely across municipalities and because the notional rental values upon which the tax is based have not been updated since the 1970s. It should be mentioned that France's reform does not affect the *taxe foncière* which will continue to be levied on the owners of immovable property.

Denmark also introduced important changes to housing taxation. From 2021, housing taxes – including both the property value tax and the land tax – will reflect property market values, thereby ending the property valuation freeze in place since 2002, which has led to falling effective tax rates for homes experiencing increases in value. For many homes, this change will lead to higher valuations. Tax rates will be lowered, however, and homeowners whose overall housing taxes increase with the new system will be compensated through a tax rebate. In an effort to protect homeowners from tax increases while they occupy their home, the payment of tax increases after 2021 will also be deferred until the home is sold.

Changes to transaction taxes on movable and immovable property were introduced in a few countries. To support homeownership among the younger generations, the United Kingdom introduced a full relief from stamp duty land tax (SDLT) for all residential property transactions of up to GBP 300 000 by first-time buyers. First-time buyers paying between GBP 300 000 and GBP 500 000 will pay SDLT at 5% on the amount of the purchase price in excess of GBP 300 000, a reduction of GBP 5 000 compared to the amount of SDLT they would have previously paid. First-time buyers purchasing property above GBP 500 000 are not entitled to any relief. Argentina repealed its 1.5% tax on the transfer of real estate and will instead apply a 15% tax on the capital gain on the sale of real estate (only for second and additional homes). On the other hand, increases in transaction taxes on immovable property were reported in Ireland, where the stamp duty on non-residential property was raised from 2% to 6%, and in the Canadian province of Ontario which introduced a Non-Resident Speculation Tax of 15% on the purchase of residential property located in the greater Toronto area by non-residents or foreign corporations. Regarding transactions of movable assets, Belgium reported an increase in the rates of its tax on stock exchange transactions.

The most significant change in the area of inheritance and gift taxes was introduced in the United States. The estate and gift tax exemption threshold was doubled to USD 10 million. This enhanced exemption applies to estates of decedents, generation-skipping transfers, and gifts made after 2017, but is subject to a sunset clause in 2025. The Joint Committee on Taxation estimated that this provision would lower revenues by USD 83 billion over 10 years. Inheritance and gift tax changes were also introduced in Luxembourg and South Africa. In Luxembourg, the exemption from inheritance tax – so far restricted to spouses or partners with at least one child – was extended to all spouses or partners engaged in a partnership of at least three years before the death of one of the partners. South Africa, on the other hand, raised taxes on wealth transfers. The duty rates on both estates and donations of more than ZAR 30 million were raised from 20% to 25% as of 1 March 2018.

As part of a broader set of reforms to encourage investment, France repealed its net wealth tax and replaced it with a tax on real estate wealth (Box 3.13). France was among the four OECD countries that still had a net wealth tax in 2017 (Box 3.14). As of 2018, the wealth tax was repealed and replaced with a tax on real estate wealth, implying a significant narrowing of the tax base which is now restricted to non-professional real estate property and excludes all financial and movable assets. The tax exemption threshold of EUR 1.3 million, the tax brackets and the 30% allowance applicable to the value of the main residence remain the same as under the wealth tax. The stated objective of this change was to support productive investment, and therefore growth, while continuing to tax wealthy households on their housing assets. In Norway, the base of the net wealth tax continued to be narrowed, in line with previous reforms seeking to reduce the wealth tax burden (OECD, 2018[43]).

Finally, Belgium introduced a new tax akin to a wealth tax on securities accounts to enhance fairness and raise revenue. Wealthy Belgian tax residents will be subject to a new annual tax of 0.15% on their Belgian and foreign securities accounts. In principle, non-resident individuals will also have to pay the tax on their Belgian securities accounts. The tax will only be due if the total average value of the securities accounts of an individual exceeds EUR 500 000. The taxable base will be equal to the total average value of the financial instruments calculated on a quarterly basis including listed and unlisted shares and bonds, shares of investment companies and units in investment funds, savings certificates and warrants. Life insurance contracts and pension savings accounts are excluded. As a rule, Belgian intermediaries (banks and brokers) will be responsible for withholding and declaring the tax.

Box 3.14. France's tax reform package

On 21 December 2017, the French Parliament adopted the Finance Act for 2018. The overall reform package has four key objectives: supporting the purchasing power of the middle class; increasing the purchasing power of workers; encouraging productive investment, through business tax reforms but also through a significant reform of personal capital taxation; and reducing the consumption of fossil fuels. Overall, the tax reform aims to reduce the level of taxes and SSCs by 1 percentage point of GDP by 2022, starting with a cut of EUR 10 billion in 2018.

On the corporate side, the CIT rate will be lowered progressively to 25% by 2022 and the 3% dividend tax, which was recently declared unconstitutional, will be repealed. In addition, the tax credit for competitiveness and employment (CICE) will be eliminated and replaced by a reduction in employer SSCs. Overall, business taxation is expected to be reduced by more than EUR 8 billion by the end of the five-year term and all types of businesses are expected to benefit from the reform.

Regarding households, the major measures to raise purchasing power include the repeal of the dwelling tax for 80% of households, viewed as unfair largely because housing values have not been updated since the 1970s, and the repeal of the health and unemployment social contributions in 2018, which will be offset by an increase in the generalised social contribution (CSG), levied on all types of income including capital and pension income.

A few measures are also aimed at rewarding risk-taking and at making the tax system more growth-friendly including the transformation of the net wealth tax into a tax on real estate wealth and the introduction of a 30% flat tax on personal capital income.

Finally, the package includes measures to encourage virtuous environmental behaviours including increases in carbon taxes and merging the tax regimes for gasoline and diesel.

Box 3.15. The evolution of net wealth taxes in OECD countries

Net wealth taxes are recurrent taxes on individual net wealth stocks. They include national and subnational recurrent taxes on a wide range of movable and immovable property, net of debt. They are distinct from other taxes on capital, including taxes on capital income and taxes on wealth transfers. They can also be distinguished from other taxes on wealth stocks: compared to recurrent taxes on immovable property, they are taxes on a broad range of property and debts are deductible; and unlike sporadic capital levies, net wealth taxes are levied on a regular basis (usually annually).

Many European OECD countries used to have net wealth taxes but repealed them in the 1990s and 2000s including Austria (in 1994), Denmark (in 1997), Germany (in 1997), the Netherlands (in 2001), Finland, Iceland, Luxembourg (all three in 2006) and Sweden (in 2007). France is the most recent country to repeal its net wealth tax, which was replaced by a tax on real estate wealth as of 2018. Norway, Spain and Switzerland are the only OECD countries that continue to levy net wealth taxes in 2018.

Evolution of the number of OECD countries levying individual net wealth taxes over time

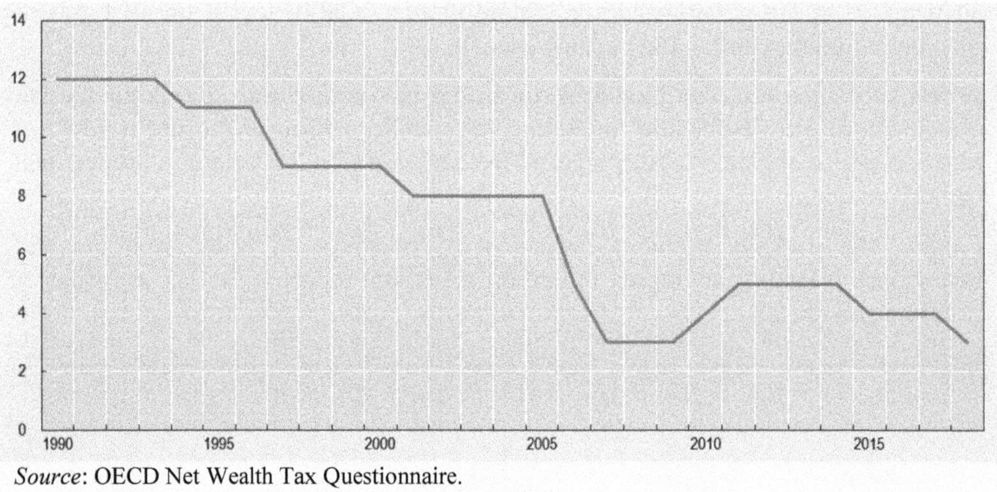

Source: OECD Net Wealth Tax Questionnaire.

Many factors have been put forward to justify the repeal of net wealth taxes. The main arguments relate to their efficiency costs and the risks of capital flight, in particular in light of increased capital mobility and wealthy taxpayers' access to tax havens; the observation that net wealth taxes often failed to meet their redistributive goals as a result of their narrow tax bases as well as tax avoidance and evasion; and concerns about their high administrative and compliance costs, in particular compared to their limited revenues (i.e. high cost-yield ratio). The repeal of net wealth taxes can also be viewed as part of a more general trend towards lowering tax rates on top income earners and capital over the past 30 years.

Source: (OECD, 2018[43])

Notes

[1] The report includes all OECD countries as at 1 January 2018.

[2] In addition to federal PIT in the United States, state PIT can be levied on top of this.

[3] In some countries, where owner-occupied homes are considered a source of income, an imputed rental income, which is subject tax, is calculated on the value of the home.

[4] Given the 24-month holding period, capital gains on the sale of shares will in practice be exempted for the first time in 2020.

[5] This average uses 28% as the standard CIT rate for France.

[6] Deemed distributions include non-business expenses, excess interest payments, transfer pricing adjustments among certain other payments.

[7] In other words, the profits distributed will be divided by 0.8 before applying the 20% rate; this implies that distributions will be taxed at a CIT effective rate of 25%.

[8] Latvian individuals receiving distributions that have been subject to the new corporate tax are not liable to any other tax on the dividends they receive.

[9] Double tax treaties typically provide for a reduced withholding tax rate of, e.g., 5% instead of the statutory 15%.

[10] To be eligible to be totally expensed, the assets must have a regular depreciation life of 20 years or less and must have been purchased after September 2017. While some types of assets are excluded by the provision, the reform has included among the eligible assets also "used properties". The asset no longer needs to be new to be eligible for full expensing, it is, however required that the taxpayer asking for the expense should not have owned the property before.

[11] The Hungarian government grants a general investment tax credit for the promotion of development; investments have to meet several qualifying conditions. The credit can be claimed over a 13-year period within the 16 years following the request; it cannot exceed 80% of taxes due.

[12] In 2017, two additional SEZs have been launched: Progreso and Salina Cruz. In total there will now be five SEZs: Coatzacoalcos, Puerto Chiapas, Salina Cruz, Lázaro Cárdenas-La Union and Progreso. These incentives apply to investments in Coatzacoalcos, Puerto Chiapas, Salina Cruz and Lázaro Cárdenas-La Union.

[13] These incentives apply only to investments in Progreso.

[14] A CFC is a foreign corporation having more than 50% of stocks (by value or vote) owned by US Shareholder. Notice that the definition of US shareholder changed due to the reform. A US shareholder is now defined as any US person (including partnerships) who owns at least 10% of a foreign corporation's stock by vote or value.

[15] Passive income includes, e.g. interest or royalties; as listed in the US Code Section 952. If such income is earned by a CFC, it is taxed as US shareholder income.

[16] This deduction will be reduced to 37.5% after 2025.

[17] Accounting for the reduced CIT rate of 21% and the 50% deduction, the GILTI included in a C-corporation's income will be taxed at 10.5%; taking the tax credit of 80% into account this implies that no residual tax liability arises if the foreign tax rate is 13.125% or higher.

[18] Foreign related parties include any 25% owner (either by voting power or by value) of the tax

payer, related person thereto, and any other person related to the taxpayer under the US transfer pricing statute.

[19] Also, they do not include payments made for routine services, qualified derivative payments and payments subject to a withholding tax in the US.

[20] For the purposes of this report the terms "value added tax" and "VAT" are used to refer to any national tax that embodies the basic features of a value added tax as described in Chapter 1 of the Guidelines, by whatever name or acronym it is known, *e.g.* "Goods and Services Tax" ("GST").

[21] The temporary increase in the Swiss standard VAT rate by 0.4 percentage points introduced in 2011 expired at the end of 2017. As of 1 January 2018, the standard VAT rate was increased by 0.1 percentage point to support the financing and expansion of the railway infrastructure.

[22] In the European Union, where there are no customs controls at the internal borders, the B2B intra-community supply of goods is VAT-free in the member state of origin and VAT is collected in the member state of destination according to a cross-border "reverse charge mechanism" where the customer in the member state of destination accounts for the VAT on the supply in its VAT return rather than paying the VAT to customs at importation. When the goods are used to make an onwards taxable transaction (e.g. a domestic supply of goods), the input VAT on this "acquisition" is entirely deductible and triggers no payment obligation. This deviates from the traditional design of a VAT, where the tax is collected through a staged collection process. Fraudsters have used this system to run "missing trader" schemes where the purchaser that has acquired the goods VAT-free resells the goods on the domestic market, collecting the VAT from its customer and vanish without remitting the VAT so collected. The same goods may be resold again several times through a network of companies across member states with a chain of VAT-free cross-border supplies, reverse charged acquisitions and resales with collection (and no remittance) of VAT creating a "carousel" fraud.

[23] This measure was taken to combat non-compliance by foreign businesses selling goods to UK consumers where the goods are in the United Kingdom (in a storage facility or "fulfilment house") at the time of sale. These sales attract UK VAT but many foreign online sellers omit to declare and pay it. As the seller is based outside the enforcement jurisdiction of the tax authorities, the latter may impose, in some circumstances, to the operator of the online marketplace through which the sale is made a joint and several liability for the VAT due in respect of the sales made by the foreign trader. This would be the case in particular when the tax authorities have warned the operator of the online marketplace of the failure of the underlying supplier to register/account for tax. This would encourage online marketplaces to "police" the underlying suppliers.

[24] Goods with a value of more than AUD 1000 will continue to be taxed upon importation according to the standard customs procedure.

[25] Since 2014, Mexico implemented a wide-ranging environmental tax and price reform, which resulted in rate and revenue increases (Arlinghaus and van Dender, 2017[31]).

[26] Based on the exchange rate in April 2018.

[27] Denmark, as part of a broader tax reform, is decreasing its registration tax for passenger cars and motorcycles, one of the highest among EU countries. In Argentina vehicle taxes are decreased by increasing the minimum tax threshold.

References

Arlinghaus, J. and K. van Dender (2017), "The environmental tax and subsidy reform in Mexico", *OECD Taxation Working Papers*, No. 31, OECD Publishing, Paris, http://dx.doi.org/10.1787/a9204f40-en. [31]

BBC (2018), "Plastic bag charge: 5p levy could be extended in England - BBC News", https://www.bbc.com/news/uk-42630898 (accessed on 16 August 2018). [41]

Dahlby, B. and E. Ferede (2012), "The effects of tax rate changes on tax bases and the marginal cost of public funds for Canadian provincial governments", *International Tax and Public Finance*, http://dx.doi.org/10.1007/s10797-012-9210-7. [5]

Dechezleprêtre, A., R. Martin and S. Bassi (2016), "Climate change policy, innovation and growth", The Grantham Research Institute on Climate Change and the Environment, London School of Economics and Political Science, http://www.lse.ac.uk/GranthamInstitute/wp-content/uploads/2016/01/Dechezlepretre-et-al-policy-brief-Jan-2016.pdf. [25]

Dechezleprêtre, A., R. Martin and M. Mohnen (2013), "Knowledge spillovers from clean and dirty technologies: A patent citation analysis", *Grantham Research Institute and the Environment Working Paper No 151*. [24]

Dressler, L., T. Hanappi and K. Van Dender (2018), "Unintended technology-bias in corporate income taxation: The case of electricity generation in the low-carbon transition", https://www.oecd-ilibrary.org/taxation/unintended-technology-bias-in-corporate-income-taxation_9f4a34ff-en (accessed on 16 August 2018). [44]

Dressler, L., T. Hanappi and K. van Dender (2018), "Unintended technology-bias in corporate income taxation: The case of electricity generation in the low-carbon transition", *OECD Taxation Working Papers*, No. 37, OECD Publishing, Paris, http://dx.doi.org/10.1787/9f4a34ff-en. [26]

European Commission (2018), *Proposal VAT Rates - European Commission*, https://ec.europa.eu/taxation_customs/business/vat/action-plan-vat/proposal-vat-rates_en (accessed on 16 August 2018). [15]

European Commission (2017), *Digital Single Market - Modernising VAT for cross border e-Commerce - European Commission*, https://ec.europa.eu/taxation_customs/business/vat/digital-single-market-modernising-vat-cross-border-ecommerce_en (accessed on 16 August 2018). [19]

Fricke, H. and B. Süssmuth (2014), "Growth and Volatility of Tax Revenues in Latin America", *World Development*, http://dx.doi.org/10.1016/j.worlddev.2013.07.007. [6]

Government of Norway (2017), *Main tax policy features – an unofficial translation of Chapter 1 of Propo. 1 LS (2017-2018)*, https://www.regjeringen.no/contentassets/c64f1881009044938c403b5236acceab/main_tax_policy_features_chapter_1.pdf (accessed on 16 August 2018). [35]

Hanappi, T. (2018), "Loss carryover provisions: Measuring effects on tax symmetry and automatic stabilisation", *OECD Taxation Working Papers*, No. 35, OECD Publishing, Paris, http://dx.doi.org/10.1787/bfbcd0db-en. [11]

Harding, M. (2014), "Personal Tax Treatment of Company Cars and Commuting Expenses: Estimating the Fiscal and Environmental Costs", *OECD Taxation Working Papers*, No. 20, OECD Publishing, Paris, http://dx.doi.org/10.1787/5jz14cg1s7vl-en. [36]

Hirst, D. (2018), *Carbon Price Floor (CPF) and the price support mechanism*, House of Commons Library, London, http://researchbriefings.files.parliament.uk/documents/SN05927/SN05927.pdf. [30]

Hogg, D. et al. (2016), *Study on Assessing the Environmental Fiscal Reform Potential for the EU28*, http://www.eunomia.co.uk (accessed on 16 August 2018). [38]

Institute for European Environmental Policy (IEEP) (2017), "New suite of 40 case studies on environmental fiscal reform", https://ieep.eu/publications/new-suite-of-40-case-studies-on-environmental-fiscal-reform (accessed on 16 August 2018). [42]

Keen, M. and K. Konrad (2013), "The theory of international tax competition and coordination", *Handbook of Public Economics*, http://dx.doi.org/10.1016/B978-0-444-53759-1.00005-4. [9]

Mahler, A. et al. (2017), *Die Finanzierung Deutschlands über Steuern auf Arbeit, Kapital und Umweltverschmutzung, Forum Ökologisch Soziale Marktwirtschaft e.V./Green Budget Germany*, http://www.foes.de/pdf/2017-06-Hintergrundpapier-Steuerstruktur.pdf. [32]

OECD (2018), *Tax Challenges Arising from Digitalisation – Interim Report 2018: Inclusive Framework on BEPS*, OECD/G20 Base Erosion and Profit Shifting Project, OECD Publishing, Paris, http://dx.doi.org/10.1787/9789264293083-en. [12]

OECD (2018), *Taxation of Household Savings*, OECD Tax Policy Studies, No. 25, OECD Publishing, Paris, http://dx.doi.org/10.1787/9789264289536-en. [3]

OECD (2018), *Taxing Energy Use 2018: Companion to the Taxing Energy Use Database*, OECD Publishing, Paris, http://dx.doi.org/10.1787/9789264289635-en. [22]

OECD (2018), *Taxing Wages 2018*, OECD Publishing, Paris, http://dx.doi.org/10.1787/tax_wages-2018-en. [1]

OECD (2018), *The Role and Design of Net Wealth Taxes in the OECD*, OECD Tax Policy Studies, No. 26, OECD Publishing, Paris, http://dx.doi.org/10.1787/9789264290303-en. [43]

OECD (2017), *Environmental Fiscal Reform Progress, Prospects and Pitfalls*, http://www.oecd.org/tax/tax-policy/tax-and-environment.htm. (accessed on 16 August 2018). [21]

OECD (2017), *Revenue Statistics: 1965-2016*, OECD Publishing, Paris, http://dx.doi.org/10.1787/9789264283183-en. [13]

OECD (2017), *Tax Policy Reforms 2017: OECD and Selected Partner Economies*, OECD Publishing, Paris, http://dx.doi.org/10.1787/9789264279919-en. [23]

OECD (2016), *Effective Carbon Rates: Pricing CO2 through Taxes and Emissions Trading Systems*, OECD Publishing, Paris, http://dx.doi.org/10.1787/9789264260115-en. [28]

OECD (2015), *Addressing the Tax Challenges of the Digital Economy, Action 1 - 2015 Final Report*, OECD/G20 Base Erosion and Profit Shifting Project, OECD Publishing, Paris, http://dx.doi.org/10.1787/9789264241046-en. [18]

OECD (2011), *Taxation and Employment*, OECD Tax Policy Studies, No. 21, OECD Publishing, Paris, http://dx.doi.org/10.1787/9789264120808-en. [2]

OECD (2010), *Tax Policy Reform and Economic Growth*, OECD Tax Policy Studies, No. 20, OECD Publishing, Paris, http://dx.doi.org/10.1787/9789264091085-en. [14]

OECD Forum on Tax Administration (2010), *Guidance for the Standard Audit File – Tax Version 2.0*, http://www.oecd.org/dataoecd/42/34/45045414.pdf (accessed on 16 August 2018). [17]

OECD/KIPF (2014), *The Distributional Effects of Consumption Taxes in OECD Countries*, OECD Tax Policy Studies, No. 22, OECD Publishing, Paris, http://dx.doi.org/10.1787/9789264224520-en. [16]

Pomerleau, K. and K. Jahnsen (2017), *Designing a Territorial Tax System: A Review of OECD Systems*, https://www. (accessed on 16 August 2018). [10]

Reuters (2018), "France calls on EU nations to adopt carbon price floor | Reuters", https://www.reuters.com/article/us-eu-carbon/france-calls-on-eu-nations-to-adopt-carbon-price-floor-idUSKBN1GH2QA (accessed on 16 August 2018). [29]

Roy, R. (2014), "Environmental and Related Social Costs of the Tax Treatment of Company Cars and Commuting Expenses", *OECD Environment Working Papers*, No. 70, OECD Publishing, Paris, http://dx.doi.org/10.1787/5jxwrr5163zp-en. [37]

Russell S. Sobel, R. (1996), "Measuring the growth and variability of tax bases over the business cycle", *National Tax Journal*. [4]

The Guardian (2017), "Norway leads way on electric cars: 'it's part of a green taxation shift' | Environment | The Guardian", https://www.theguardian.com/environment/2017/dec/25/norway-leads-way-electric-cars-green-taxation-shift (accessed on 16 August 2018). [34]

United Kingdom Department for Environment, F. (2017), *Single-use plastic carrier bags charge: data in England for 2016 to 2017 - GOV.UK*, https://www.gov.uk/government/publications/carrier-bag-charge-summary-of-data-in-england/single-use-plastic-carrier-bags-charge-data-in-england-for-2016-to-2017 (accessed on 16 August 2018). [40]

Van Dender, K. (2018), "Taxing vehicles, fuel and road use: what mix for road transport? (forthcoming)", *OECD Taxation Working Papers*. [27]

Vos, H. (2017), *Environmental tax reform (ETR): some proposals and intentions in the Netherlands for 2018 and beyond* |, https://green-budget.eu/environmental-tax-reform-etr-some-proposals-and-intentions-in-the-netherlands-for-2018-and-beyond/ (accessed on 16 August 2018). [33]

Watkins, E. (2012), *Use of Economic Instruments and Waste Management Performances: Final Report European Commission (DG ENV) Unit G.4 Sustainable Production and Consumption*, http://ec.europa.eu/environment/waste/strategy.htm (accessed on 16 August 2018). [39]

Wilson, J. (1986), "A theory of interregional tax competition", *Journal of Urban Economics*, http://dx.doi.org/10.1016/0094-1190(86)90045-8. [7]

World Health Organization (2015), *WHO report on the global tobacco epidemic: Raising taxes on tobacco*, http://dx.doi.org/ISBN 978 92 4 069460 6. [20]

Zodrow, G. and P. Mieszkowski (1986), "Pigou, Tiebout, property taxation, and the underprovision of local public goods", *Journal of Urban Economics*, http://dx.doi.org/10.1016/0094-1190(86)90048-3. [8]

ORGANISATION FOR ECONOMIC CO-OPERATION AND DEVELOPMENT

The OECD is a unique forum where governments work together to address the economic, social and environmental challenges of globalisation. The OECD is also at the forefront of efforts to understand and to help governments respond to new developments and concerns, such as corporate governance, the information economy and the challenges of an ageing population. The Organisation provides a setting where governments can compare policy experiences, seek answers to common problems, identify good practice and work to co-ordinate domestic and international policies.

The OECD member countries are: Australia, Austria, Belgium, Canada, Chile, the Czech Republic, Denmark, Estonia, Finland, France, Germany, Greece, Hungary, Iceland, Ireland, Israel, Italy, Japan, Korea, Latvia, Lithuania, Luxembourg, Mexico, the Netherlands, New Zealand, Norway, Poland, Portugal, the Slovak Republic, Slovenia, Spain, Sweden, Switzerland, Turkey, the United Kingdom and the United States. The European Union takes part in the work of the OECD.

OECD Publishing disseminates widely the results of the Organisation's statistics gathering and research on economic, social and environmental issues, as well as the conventions, guidelines and standards agreed by its members.

OECD PUBLISHING, 2, rue André-Pascal, 75775 PARIS CEDEX 16
(23 2018 36 1 P) ISBN 978-92-64-30445-1 – 2018

www.ingramcontent.com/pod-product-compliance
Ingram Content Group UK Ltd.
Pitfield, Milton Keynes, MK11 3LW, UK
UKHW051506290926
15471UKWH00008B/1456

9 789264 304451